ORIGINAL MONOLOGS THAT SHOWCASE YOUR TALENT

Dwight Watson

ALLWORTH PRESS
NEW YORK

© 2005 Dwight Watson

08 07 06 05 04   5 4 3 2 1

Published by Allworth Press
An imprint of Allworth Communications, Inc.
10 East 23rd Street, New York, NY 10010

Cover design by Derek Bacchus

Cover and interior photographs by James Gross

Interior design by Mary Belibasakis

Page composition/typography by Integra Software Services, Pvt., Ltd., Pondicherry, India

ISBN–1-58115-425-9

Library of Congress Cataloging-in-Publication Data

Watson, Dwight, 1952.
    Original monologs that showcase your talent/Dwight Watson.
        p.   cm.
    Includes index.
    ISBN 1-58115-425-9 (pbk.)
1. Monologues.   2. Acting.   I. Title.

PN2080.W38 2005
812'.6—dc22

                                                                    2005015557

Printed in Canada

CONTENTS

ACKNOWLEDGEMENTS

IT IS WITH SINCERE GRATITUDE that I acknowledge those who helped to bring this book to completion. While writing these monologs, I enjoyed encouragement from family, friends, students, and colleagues. Special acknowledgement belongs to my theater department colleagues at Wabash College: James Fisher, Mike Abbott, Laura Conners, and James Gross. I am also grateful to Wabash College for enabling me to complete much of this work during a sabbatical and with Wabash College Faculty Development grant support. I am fortunate to work with many talented and energetic students in rehearsal and in the classroom. These students are a reliable source of inspiration. In preparing the manuscript for publication, I am indebted to my editor, Nicole Potter-Talling and to the entire Allworth staff for their valuable assistance, guidance, and professionalism. Lastly, I wish to thank my wife, Jamie, and my sons, Matthew and Evan. I depend on Jamie's kindness, talent, and unreserved honesty, and I am most grateful that she has passed these traits on to Matthew and Evan. This book is dedicated to them.

INTRODUCTION

ONCE THESPIS, THE FIRST ACTOR, stepped out of the Greek chorus in 534 B.C., the exchange of language, or *dialogue*, became a key element in the evolution of drama. The importance of dialogue, and, particularly, the rapid *stichomythia*, as the Greeks called it—the fast back-and-forth interplay of language—created the necessity of multiple voices in drama, and the poet became a playwright aware of the collaborative nature of performing art. When we think of a theatrical monolog, however, we generally think of a long speech performed by one onstage character, a speech in which the action of the play slows down to accommodate the solo voice. We value dialogue in our lives; we prize good dialogic discussion in the classroom and workplace, and we are suspicious of the individual who launches into a monolog, excluding others with his solipsistic view of the world. However, the good theatrical monolog is an extension of dialogue; you might even call it an imaginary dialogue offered in one voice.

A distinct monolog form is one in which the character speaking directs his or her language to an imaginary character on stage. This form, by necessity or design, is most often used by actors in auditions, or simply as a means for character study. The monologs in this book employ an imaginary character, yet each monolog exists as an independent short story with a beginning, middle, and end. In this way, I hope these monologs remain essentially one-person plays. Furthermore, each monolog is crafted to allow the actor an opportunity to show a range of emotion while showcasing a particular talent (e.g., tap-dancing, jumping rope, skateboarding, playing drums, etc.).

In an effort to add a foundation (or maybe a diversion) while creating these monologs, I studied historical and biographical information about the celebrated physicist Sir Isaac Newton (1642–1727). Consequently, the "unseen character" in this collection is often referred to as Newton or Newt. Much is known about Sir Isaac Newton's brilliant work in physics and mathematics, but while preparing this collection of monologs, I first became intrigued by a quote often attributed to the scientist:

⁂

> I do not know what I may appear to the world, but to myself I seem to have been only like a boy playing on the sea-shore, and diverting myself in now and then finding a smoother pebble or a prettier shell than ordinary, whilst the great ocean of truth lay all undiscovered before me.

⁂

Here, I thought, was the beginning of Sir Isaac Newton's autobiography, a personal monolog that suggests a high degree of playfulness instead of the strictly logical mind one generally associates with the man who laid the foundations for modern science. Further study of Sir Isaac suggests that he may have been a rather quirky fellow, inclined to immerse himself in his experiments, often to physical extremes. For example, it is reported that he stared at the sun beyond reasonable tolerance so that he could record what would happen to his vision. Newton was a passionate seeker of knowledge in the fields of mathematics, optics, and physics, but also in the "ocean of truth" he saw in magic, alchemy, and theology.

The Newton is this monolog collection is often the unseen character who creates tension or serves as an unusual sounding board. He might be a good listener, a thoughtful observer, an accompanist, a mass of energy, or a dog chasing seagulls on the beach. Sometimes Newton appears as bits and pieces of Sir Isaac Newton's life and work. For example, Sir Isaac's *Principia*, his books on the laws of motion and gravity, become Princess Ipia in the monolog *Birth of a Star*. It is most important to know that the name is somewhat arbitrary in this monolog collection, and at best, the Newton "character" serves as an invisible force. To connect these monologs to the science of theoretical physics would take an act of extreme imagination. It is not, however, too much of a stretch to believe that Newton's laws of motion also apply to drama. We know that good drama is action—wherein a character in a state of equilibrium (or rest) is compelled to change by the actions (or the force) of another character. The character's life becomes the acceleration of unwanted or unexpected events, a journey that has the power to transport the character as well as the actor and audience from one curious place to another. It is a dramatic law of motion I wish to achieve, and I hope you will find in this work.

1 PREPPING A MONOLOG FOR PERFORMANCE

THERE IS AN OLD LITERARY CARTOON featuring the novelist Charles Dickens. I do not recall the artist, but I do recall that there are three frames to the cartoon. The first shows Dickens sitting at his desk, presumably writing a novel. The second frame again places him at his desk writing, but this time many of his fictional characters float in the ether above him. The third frame reveals a simple grave marker with "R.I.P. Dickens." He has departed from this life, and yet his characters still exist and drift in the air above him, or, more accurately, above his grave marker.

I like to imagine there is another dimension, another world, inhabited by all the great dramatic characters. I like to think of them interacting, perhaps waiting in a green room somewhere. You know these characters. They are exceptional. Some are comical, others poignant, but all are expressive, well defined, and in harmony with the scripted worlds in which they live. They are more perfect than their creators; after all, they have the power to exist long after the death of their makers. They float in this dramatic ether. It isn't all hugs and kisses in this green room, however; there is at least one drawback, one proviso in their bid for character immortality. Their existence depends on the kindness of "strange" actors.

Now, I say "strange" actors because actors, like playwrights, are temporary and imperfect (although I've met a few who would argue that point and, admittedly, I have seen a few whom I thought were really perfect), and yet they possess a remarkable desire to imagine a life of fiction—to inhabit the pretense of a character—emoting as if the imagined character's pain and joy were theirs. The codependent relationship between an actor and character may lead to an exciting characterization for the gifted actor in a fully realized production. But there are some actors, awkward, ill prepared, yet eager to pursue their mimetic instincts, who insist on acting the great dramatic characters they might best leave alone. I imagine the ethereal Blanche Dubois in *A Streetcar Named Desire* saying to one such actor, "No, no, I'm much younger than you, more beautiful; I'm all poetry and music, a fragile moth, and you make me look and sound like a squeaky rodent. Please, don't take me out there, please! Don't turn on the stage lights!" Blanche is irresistible and, as long as actors are driven by the music of the spoken word, her reincarnation on the stage is certain.

One might argue that characters are impervious and are accustomed to being violated. And because they are exceptional, actors, and maybe, secretly, all of us, want to get near them, to slip inside their unique form and play out their inspired actions. These characters become, quite naturally, the targets for actors looking for audition material—the monolog.

Most actors would agree that the audition is a nasty procedure, cruel and unusual, designed to evoke high anxieties and nervousness. It is a snippet, a splinter performance (if you dare call it a performance), where the first and finest impressions are remembered and rewarded with the role. Careful preparation for an audition and selection of appropriate audition material is crucial for any actor wishing to deliver the finest impression.

This collection of monologs attempts to address two essential ideas for actors selecting and preparing a monolog: 1) to communicate a complete character within a limited time period, and

2) to encourage the use of original and appropriate material for scene study and for the audition.

To achieve a good story monolog—a monolog with a clear beginning, middle, and end—the amount of spoken language extends beyond the time generally allotted to actors in an audition; therefore, such monologs are not appropriate pieces for auditioning. This collection contains both complete story monologs with playing times ranging from three to six minutes and edited one-minute versions.

As you read the collection, you may also be looking for a monolog or audition material that will excite and inspire a performance. The monolog should be well suited to your talents and, after serious study and memorization, it should fit as comfortably as a well-worn but still attractive sweater. I have written these monologs, but I want you to possess them. To do so, consider the following important points as you perform:

POINT 1 Know whom you are talking to. Why is the character saying what she is saying? What does she want? Study the following chapter for character objective and story synopsis.

POINT 2 Study the shape of the monolog. Honor the "architecture" of rising and falling action with appropriate voice and movement.

POINT 3 Imagine the "unseen character." Bounce your character's ideas off of the "unseen character," imagine his response, and allow genuine vocal and physical reaction to occur (even if it's as small a physical change as shifting your gaze).

POINT 4 Locate the "unseen character" or imaginary partner. In most cases, and depending on the performance space, the imaginary partner should exist beyond the auditioner, while you keep your face lifted and visible. For a stage audition or a taped audition, usually choose to place the partner slightly to the right or left of the lens.

Point 5 Make clear emotional, vocal, and physical choices. Be well prepared and confident!

Point 6 Integrate your talent into the preparation of monolog. Many of the monologs in this collection allow you to showcase acting skills and special techniques, such as tap dancing in *Hoofer*, jumping rope in *Ode to Little Audrey*, or riding a skateboard in *Shorty's Old Man's Board or S'up?*.

Finally, enjoy the opportunity to share your talent with others. Listen to the great Italian actress Eleonora Duse (1858–1924) and her words of encouragement:

❈ · ❈ · ❈

The artist-actor gives the best of himself; through his interpretations he unveils his inner soul. By these interpretations only should he be accepted and judged. When the final curtain falls between him and his audience, nothing can be said or done, add or detract from his performance. His work is done, his message is delivered.

❈ · ❈ · ❈

As you prep a monolog for performance, you will go through periods during which you feel alone, unnaturally talking to yourself. As a writer, I have experienced similar moments. But when you add an audience, the solo performance or audition takes on a special quality, an unusual intimacy. As you act you may be directing your energy to an "unseen character," but the invisible force of the audience is always presence. Enjoy that connection.

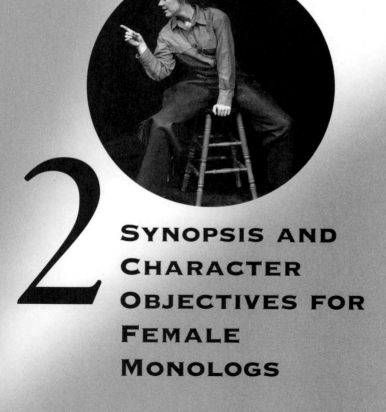

2

SYNOPSIS AND
CHARACTER
OBJECTIVES FOR
FEMALE
MONOLOGS

PRINCESS IPIA—*Birth of a Star*

As an employee of a local florist, this nineteen-year-old woman is delivering a "break-a-leg" bouquet for Julie Snow, star of the Ice Capades. The delivery girl is also a fan, and she and her father have tickets for the show. When there is no one in the office to receive the flowers, the young woman discovers a skater rehearsing on the ice. The delivery girl explains her purpose for being at the rink but goes further to reveal her identity as daughter of a former skater—her mother. It is clear that this young woman will attend tonight's performance to recapture an evening with her mother.

ALISSA—*Bon Voyage*

Alissa's current summer employment as a lifeguard is a pimple on the butt of her summer. Clearly the only thing to be gained from this job is enough money for her summer trip to Paris. She is eager to stomp through this last day on the job to discover her true identity—that French-speaking woman-of-the-world sipping wine on the Champs Elysées.

ZENITH BLACKETER—*Hoofer*

In her fertile imagination, Zenith sees herself tapping her way to Broadway—this generation's Ruby Keeler or Ann Miller, the female version of Gregory Hines—if only she could get her first break. As is true with most hopeful performers, human frailties interfere with her rise to stardom.

JULIE STALBIRD—*Tractors and Twirlers*

An otherwise casual spectator, Julie has actually come to witness the Thanksgiving parade to reassure herself that she is, of course, more talented and skillful than any of Mrs. Troutman's Twirlers.

AUDREY—*Ode to Little Audrey*

A quick wit and skilled rope jumper, Audrey keeps moving and talking so that she doesn't have to think or feel.

SHELLEY—*Hummers, Rockets, and Split Comets*

Shelley is in love with romance itself. A beautiful starry Fourth of July night, a secret location, and a lover's rendezvous between Cary Grant (Newton, her boyfriend) and Grace Kelly (Shelley). Her evening will be complete when Cary (Newton) arrives—or maybe anticipation is better than realization.

SARAH—$F = Wd$

It is exam week and Sarah, a focused, high-strung science major, is looking for a target at which to aim her test anxiety. When a dorm mate accuses Sarah of trying to steal the girl's boyfriend, she provides the necessary trigger, and Sarah unleashes her anger and frustration.

NICOLE—*Stage Fright Pianologue*

A talented pianist, Nicole's dream is to accompany singers and to share her talent. Her obstacle is a debilitating phobia—stage fright. Nicole seeks affirmation as she employs various strategies to overcome the phobia, share her talent, and find rewarding employment.

KATIE BELLE—*Buckaroo Belle and the Bull Rider*

Heedless of the gender differences in the male-dominated sport of competitive bull riding, Katie Belle shares her excitement and knowledge of the sport while asserting her rightful place among the best riders.

VIRGINIA DARE—*Chocolate Thin Mints*

To Virginia, the only thing worse than a Yankee in a prestigious Southern college is a thin, attractive Yankee who eats whatever she pleases and flaunts the fact that she never gains an ounce. Virginia's objective is clear—she must evict her roommate. In order to accomplish this, she must enlist the support of the Director of Residential Life. She will not take no for an answer.

TORRIE—*The Twilight Arch*

Torrie and a friend have climbed a ridge to look at the night sky and to listen for the howling of coyotes. Torrie carries with her a secret that is about to cause her to implode. She has suppressed it too long, and now must share it.

LIZZIE—*Lizzie's Lilliput*

Obsessed with an uncontrollable desire to talk (mainly about herself), Lizzie, a young college student, struggles to find friendship as well as her identity on campus.

KARI—*Two Blushing Pilgrims*

Kari, a costume and makeup assistant for a production of *Romeo and Juliet*, sees the stage manager for the first time since they were "together" the previous night. Kari masks her embarrassment and feelings of vulnerability with a run-on monolog of insignificant theatrical details regarding the cast and production. Finally, she exhausts the trivia talk, and lets slip her genuine feelings for the stage manager.

DARCY WELLS—*Hard Knocks*

Darcy uses her theatrical heritage, training, and experience as a shield to protect herself from a recent casting disappointment at a local theater. As a theatrical "lifer," she freely shares her expertise as other young actors audition for the title character in a production of *Annie*.

CHARLOTTA—*Head Shot and Hot Buttered Biscuits*

Although Charlotta is a newcomer to the stage, her worldly perspective and natural honest instincts make her a genuine performer. Only when she assumes the technical trappings of theater does she appear stilted and out of sync. Like any good actor, Charlotta knows how to connect with her audience in order to reveal her soul. Now she seeks validation and a real career, and so solicits help from a professional director.

RENEE—*Beast Ballet*

Short on members of the *corps de ballet*, Renee, a serious ballet student, attempts to make a dancer out of a knock-kneed, hairy "sow's ear." Assuming that the new recruit should share her passion, Renee attempts to remake her student in her image.

3

SYNOPSIS AND
CHARACTER
OBJECTIVES FOR
MALE MONOLOGS

Otto Gunther—*A Lean, Mean, Singing Machine*
Although not what some might call a "typical" choral director, Otto Gunther has an unyielding passion for singing great music well. His method is not to coax or conjure, but to "light a fire," so that choral members hold nothing back.

Joel—*Peter Pan and the Square-rigger*
Having no ship to sail, Joel and his crew have been asked to share their expertise to assist with a production of *Peter Pan*. Joel, a kind-hearted but take-charge sailor, seizes this opportunity to employ his skills as the stage becomes a ship.

Allen—*A Seamless Pitch*
Allen has invited Angela, an exchange student from Africa, to skip stones, but his real purpose is to find a private opportunity to express his feelings for her.

1ˢᵀ Dead Man—*The 1st Dead Man in Grover's Corners*
In a rehearsal for *Our Town*, the actor playing George has missed his cue. The actor playing the 1ˢᵗ Dead Man seizes the

opportunity to spew—he bombards the director with his assessment of the production.

ADAM—*Dodgeball Matador*

Adam is tired of being a target. Today he digs deep to summon his courage. He rises above the crass, sweaty atmosphere of the gym to become a matador.

GEORGE BOTTOM—*Bottom's Dream*

If George were a betting man, he would stack all his chips on the arm of a young pitcher on the mound. "Vicarious" doesn't begin to explain George. He exists within the game and, of course, he knows better than the umpire. He thinks it's all up to him, and he must win the game from his seat in the stands.

HENRI—*Fie Upon't!*

Henri begins with good intentions, attempting to encourage a fellow actor, but the mask soon slips and finally falls entirely to reveal Henri's resentment. He believes the role should be his!

MITCHELL GRAY—*Rein in the Sterling Sphinxes*

Mitchell believes that he and his friend have created the perfect float. Now Mitchell's job is to highlight every feature for the judges and to win first prize.

BARRY GASCON—*The Line-up*

Barry makes it clear that he is not participating in the audition by choice. He has heard stories about the theater and he asserts in no uncertain terms that he does not belong to the "drama club."

SLICK—*Shorty's Old Man's Board or S'up?*

Slick is chillin' with his friend. Skateboarders share a special bond as outcasts, risk takers who are indignant with the skittish limitations of the mainstream, but even Slick insists they should avoid suicide when he does all he can to prevent his friend from skateboarding down a dangerous hill.

ROSEN—*Styling with William*
Purging himself of the frustration he feels as a result of a contentious professor/student relationship, Rosen discovers a point of intersection between himself and Hamlet, and Shakespeare's words burst forth as if they were his own.

EDDIE HALLEY—*Halley's Fat Strat*
As Eddie checks the microphones for an upcoming concert, he relives his failure at school and plays out his guitarist fantasy at the mic.

THURSTON—*The Big Bang*
A soulful musician, Thurston has been harnessed and straight-jacketed into a tuxedo to play in a state orchestra. Throughout this experience, he moves from doubt and disdain for fellow musicians to total immersion in the performance to the climax of his own contribution, and satisfaction and respect for the performers.

TONY—*The Piano Tuner*
Tony has finished his job tuning the piano, but is reluctant to leave the theater. Teresa, his deceased sister, was an actress, and his presence in the theater makes him feel close to her. Tony is proud of Teresa and he misses her. In his conversation with the technical director, he finds an opportunity to share her memory and his respect for her talent and her art.

4 Monologs for Women

BIRTH OF A STAR

Scene

An ice-skating rink. A nineteen-year-old delivery girl, with a flower arrangement in her hands, makes her way to edge of the skating rink. She is quiet as she studies and admires a lone skater on the ice. After a moment and with some hesitation, she calls out to the skater.

PRINCESS IPIA: Hello! Hi! (*With friendly apology*) I don't mean to bother you, but no one was out front in the box office to take the delivery. Don't let me stop you from your figure eights. (*Admiringly*) Ohh. Just keep on skating. I just want to make sure these get delivered. I'm from Newton's Floricultural Shop. That's right, Newton's Floricultural. "We specialize in thornless long-stem roses." (*With self-conscious laughter*) I'm supposed to say that. I work there part-time to help pay for my courses at the community college. (*Placing the flowers on the floor*)

These are for Julie Snow . . . you know, the amazing skater with the Ice Capades? (*Barely able to contain her joy*) Yeah. They are a "break a leg" from an admirer. These flowers. I don't know, do you say "break a leg" to an ice skater? (*With growing excitement*) I assume you know her . . . I mean . . . of course, you know her . . . you are probably rehearsing yourself . . . for the show . . . so . . . I know you probably know her. (*Nodding her head*) Right? And you know she's skating the role of Cinderella tonight.

We come every year but it seems I've been waiting a long time for this one. I bought my tickets two months ago. (*Locating her seat*) I'm right there. In the middle, Row J, for Julie, Seat 19, which happens to be how old I am today, nineteen, and I might add that the nineteenth letter in the alphabet is "S" for Snow, and so I guess you can see that I'm just a little bit excited. Ohh. (*Slight laughter*) And my dad has the seat next to me, 20, on the aisle. Believe it or not, he is even a bigger fan. With good reason. Julie Snow reminds him of my mother. Oh, yes. (*Proudly*) My mom was a competitive skater in her twenties, but a knee injury ended all of that. Ohhh. (*Enjoying the reminiscence*) My dad said he fell in love with Mother the first time he saw her on the ice . . . figure skating. He used to say, "Princess Ipia"—that's what he calls me—"you could search the universe inside and out and you would never see anything more beautiful than your mother on skates. She was air and grace, a beautiful blur in motion," he said. And the first time he saw her pirouette and then begin to twirl . . . like they do . . . spinning faster and faster and faster, tucking her arms, collapsing in on herself, he thought he was watching the . . . birth of a star. (*Pauses*) My mother. (*Smiling*) Did I tell you she looked just like Julie Snow? (*Thoughtfully*) I was very small. Too small to know . . . her. A blur in motion. I remember the flowers though. The birth of a star. (*Pauses*) Ahh.

(*With growing delight*) On Sundays, when Dad wasn't too busy, we would go to the rink . . . and we would pretend to be world-class skaters . . . the two of us . . . a pair. Ahh. We'd go through all the motions trying to find some rhythm and harmony. (*Demonstrating with an outstretched arm*) Hand in hand . . . in circles, and then the Kilian position with my body tucked next to his, and finally when it seemed we achieved a small degree of ease on the ice, he would lean down to me and say, "Princess Ipia, are you ready to waltz?" And I would say, "Yes," knowing, of course, that the two of us waltzing on skates was not a reality. And then, my dad would whisper, "Well . . . just close your eyes, Princess, and imagine." And we would waltz. (*Pauses; she feels somewhat exposed and embarrassed*)

I need to go back to work. I didn't mean to stay so long. (*Drawing breath*) I have another delivery to make. (*Slight pause*) So . . . I will leave the flowers here. And when you see her, Julie Snow, please tell her these are from admirers.

End of Scene

Chapter 4

Bon Voyage

Scene

A public beach. Alissa, a lifeguard, dressed in swimsuit with a whistle and surrounded by her necessary sun gear (zinc salve for her nose, suntan lotion, hairbrush, towel, etc.), is near the end of her watch. She talks to her friend about a pending trip to Paris while keeping one eye on those swimming and playing in the water.

Alissa: (*Whistling loudly*) Hey! Hey! You've gone too far. Hey! (*Whistling and shouting*) You can't go past the red buoys. (*Waving him back, she then turns to her friend nearby*) Hannah, are you packed? All ready to go? I'm just so excited I've been packed for a week. I'm just so glad I took French instead of German, aren't you? I just can't wait to sip French wine and dine at one of those little sidewalk cafes on the Champs Elysées. It's the dream of my life . . . to travel . . . to Paris, France, on the continent of Europe. I can hear it now: This captivating waiter will saddle up to the table and say, *"Encore un peu de viande?"* "A little more meat?" And I'll say, *"Volontiers, monsieur, mais un tout petit morceau, je vous prie."* "Yes, thank you; but a very small piece, please." His eyes sparkle at the sight of mine, which are wide open . . . inviting him to . . . Hey! (*To the swimmer*) You're out too far! (*Whistling*) You're out too far! Ah, Christ! I should've taken that job at the Beefy Mart. This is too much stress.

(*To Hannah*) Who was that . . . that *American in Paris*, Hannah? You know the film we saw in French II? Was it Audrey Hepburn? No, no, I think she was the one in that *Roman Holiday* movie we watched in Western Civ. (*She whistles to the swimmer*) I know you can hear me! And you can hear this whistle! (*She blows*) I will not go in after you, dork! I am not going in there! So, just put it in reverse, Captain! (*To Hannah*) Well sure, I've been practicing my French. It gets pretty bad out here watching fat kids bob up and down and their sweaty parents who stir just long enough to pee in the water. They're all sea monsters. Especially that one. (*To the swimmer*) This side! Get on this side of the red buoys!

(*To Hannah*) All morning I've been working on *les parties du corps*, "the parts of my body." (*She points to her head:*) *La tête*, (*her hair*) *les cheveux*, (*her nose*) *le nez*, (*her waist*) *la taille*, (*her thigh*) *la cuisse*, (*her leg*) *la jambe*, (*her foot*) *le pied*, (*her thumb*) *le pouce. Ce va bien, non?* I'm so excited. I can't wait to speak a foreign language in a foreign country and order chicken. I still just laugh out loud when I think about what you said the other day: "We will storm the Bastille, dance barefoot in fountains, and climb Eiffel's Tower, (*Whispering*) if he lets us. (*Blowing her whistle*)

That does it! Out of the water! Hannah, do you know who that is out there? Wait a minute. Where's Newton?! I don't see him . . . so it must be . . . Newton! It's Newton! Damn him! (*Picking up a megaphone*) I know it's you, Newton. Get back here. Just paddle your fanny back to shore, and I mean now! I'm going to count to three and then I'm going to call the authorities. *Un!* Turn around, Newton. *Deux!* Do you hear me? I will not swim out there! I will not! I'm off duty in two minutes, my hair is dry, my back is peeling, and I'm going to Paris tomorrow! I am walking away from here! I'm walking away, Newton! *Trois!* Okay, go ahead. Sail away. *Au revoir*, idiot, *bon voyage* and see if I care. (*She throws up her middle finger*) *Le doigt*, dork! (*To Hannah*) Hannah, are you taking a hairdryer?

End of Scene

HOOFER

Scene

A few scattered chairs and maybe a piano are found on what is otherwise an empty stage. Auditions are taking place in the theater, although at the moment all participants are at lunch. Zenith Blacketer steps on the stage and looks out into the theater at her friend, Newton. Zenith, a tap dancer, is taking this opportunity to warm up before her dance audition.

ZENITH BLACKETER: (*To Newton*) Are you sure it's okay if we practice here? (*Looking to see if they are alone*) I know everyone else is at lunch. And I know it's a good idea to practice where the audition will take place, when it's possible. I like this floor and all. It's ideal for tap. (*Somewhat nervously*) Are you sure we're alone? I get loud sometimes and people don't like it. Some people just don't understand. But that's what tap is. Loud and snappy, and that's me! (*Dropping her shoulder bag*) But I don't want to get you in trouble, Newton. Well, that's good. (*Flattering*) You're a prince, Newton . . . a scholar . . . and a gentleman. (*Rhythmically, she sings*) Be-dee-bop, be-dee-bop, be-dee-bop! (*Catching her breath*) Whew!

I'm feeling a little lightheaded. I didn't eat before I came here. Did you? I don't like to dance on a full stomach. And since my audition is at two, I thought I could make it through. But I don't know. (*Singing*) Be-dee-dee-bop, be-dee-dee-bop, be-dee-dee-bop! Be-dee-bop! Be-dee-bop! That's just one of my little warm-ups, one of my drills. I need to sing the rhythm before I tap it, Newton. Tap is all mathematics and rhythm, but I don't count, no way, I sing. Forget the numbers and give me the sounds. (*Singing*) Be-Dee-de-Dee-bop! Be-dee-bop! Be-dee-bop. Be-Dee-de-Dee-bop! Be-dee-bop!

Do you have that sheet music I gave you? That's right, "Sweet Georgia Brown." A tapping classic. (*Reaching for her shoulder bag*) I have another copy here in my bag if you forgot it. (*She sits, rummages through her bag, and retrieves various items*) Let me see . . . well . . . here's my bottled water. What did we do before bottled water, Newton? I guess we were just a sweaty nation of dehydrated hoofers. A bag of chips. Well, maybe just one or twooooo, while I'm looking. (*Munching on chips*) Here are my tap shoes. God, Newton, I wish they could make a better shoe. We can make little sheep and transplant hearts but we can't make a tap shoe. (*Agitated*) The taps and straps fall off, and would it hurt to give us just a little more cushion on the heel, Shoe Man? Art doesn't have to be torture! (*Singing*) Be-dee-bop-bop-spank! Spank! Be-dee-bop! I mean, tap is entertainment, there's no message here. If I wanted to send a message—I'd dance modern or the grand ballet. Enough with this suffering artist crap! Give me comfort! And maybe . . . this candy bar . . . for just a little energy . . . and a few more chips. (*Ripping into the food*)

Oh, Newton, I hate to audition. It's so hard. And I already know the outcome. (*Reeling from insecurity*) She won't cast me; I just know it! I won't even make it in the chorus. And I know what she's thinking. (*With growing anxiety*) I'm not the right . . . size . . . my thighs are too big or they're too small . . . I'm too tall . . . or short. I don't have the right shape . . . or name . . . or . . . religion . . . or birth date . . . or zip code . . . or sexual orientation . . . or parents . . . or . . . insurance . . . or pet . . . or maybe she's still angry with me because of that damn stupid production of *Oklahoma*! (*A loud confession*) I didn't mean to kick Curly in the head during final dress, Newton. It was an accident! (*Knowingly*) And I think he just pretended to be in a coma so he didn't have to work with her anymore!

I'm a hoofer, for crying out loud, Newton! And a hoofer moves! (*Her emotions are spilling over*) And I'm hungry! And I don't know why I have to suffer! It won't have anything to do with my talent for tap. No. I will walk on stage, (*Demonstrating*) say my name . . . "Zenith Blacketer" . . . and before I finish saying, "This afternoon I am dancing to a tap classic, 'Sweet Georgia Brown,'" she'll say, *"Next!"* That's right, Newton, *"Next!"* I won't even get a chance to dance! No! She'll never see me tap! Well, that's just too bad. It is her loss! I'm part of an American institution, Newton. I am Ruby Keeler and Shirley Temple, rolled into one . . . I am Zenith Blacketer . . . and I have tap in my blood. Loud and snappy! (*Singing and tapping with excess emotion*) Spank! Spank! Dee-dee-dee-Dee-Bop!

End of Scene

TRACTORS AND TWIRLERS

Scene

A sidewalk on Main Street during the annual Thanksgiving parade. Julie Stalbird, a high-school student, talkative and impulsive, watches the parade with her friend, Newton. Julie's excitement matches the festive atmosphere.

JULIE STALBIRD: (*A ringing endorsement*) I love a parade. (*To Newton*) My dad said a parade "is top-choice America." And he thinks the Thanksgiving parade is "America cut thick and prime." (*Laughing*) Well, I don't know about that. I mean, I'm not a big meat eater, Newton, but I do love a parade. (*Spotting a friend*)

Hey, is that Harley Dare on his hog? Hi Harley, hi! (*To Newton*) I don't know why they call 'em . . . hogs. Do you? (*Waving frantically*) Hi Harley! I want you to give me a ride some day, Harley . . . on your hog. (*Feigning embarrassment*) God, Newton, I can't believe I just shouted that out like that. So the whole town could hear. I have a problem, blurting things out. My dad says it's because I don't think . . . first. Well, that might be . . . but I don't think you should go around suppressing your feelings. (*With growing confidence*) You've just got to let 'em out, Newton. Well, not you, Newton, I mean, me. I've got to let them out. If I keep them bottled up, I'll just explode. (*Unreservedly*) I mean, ka-bluey! Like a bomb, tick, tick, tick, ka-bluey!

(*Disgustedly*) Here we go. Tractors. Yipee. I just wish this town could organize a parade just once without tractors. It makes no sense to me. And, oh, oh, wouldn't you know, here comes the Pork Queen, Rita—Rita Wright. (*Calling out*) Hi, Rita! You look beautiful! And nice hair, too. You want to go to the Shawnee Lanes on Saturday night? I'll give you a call. (*Confiding to Newton*) Do you know Rita, Newton? Well, she's nice enough, but she's no Pork Queen. It's all who you know, you know. And her father owns Wright Farm Implements. And ... well ... everybody owes and knows Mr. Wright and so ... dot, dot, dot.

(*Shocked and near the point of tears*) Oh, no, oh, God ... here they come ... Newton ... the Twirlers. I'm not sure I can stand it. Daddy told me I would have to face this sooner or later ... but I just ... hurt ... so much ... and I'm still ... so angry. (*Sitting down*) I'm going to sit down right here, grip the curb, and try my best to keep from bursting. (*Almost hysterical*) Oh, God. Look at them ... twirl. I twirled for eight years, Newton. I'm good. (*With growing indignation*) I have trophies to prove it! I've twirled all over, all over the place. I have. I have a certificate that says, "Julie Stalbird twirled at Disney World!" At Disney World, Newton! And then ... this ... Mrs. Troutman took over the Twirlers and cut me from the team. She cut me deep, Newton. And it's not fair! I should lead ... the Twirlers ... and ... I just can't stand it ... anymore! It's just not fair! (*Shouting out*) Mrs. Troutman ... you are a fascist! A Martha Stewart wannabe! You and your perfect squad! Your perfect squad ... of size-six, five-foot-three twirlers ... all looking very ... slim ... and very ... much ... alike! This is America, Mrs. Troutman! We ... welcome ... diversity! (*Sighing*)

There. (*Collecting herself*) I feel better now. I just had to let it go. I just had to fling that thing up into the air and just let it twirl away. And I'm not ashamed, Newton, because I want Mrs. Troutman and all of her little Twirlers to feel my pain. Happy Thanksgiving. There. Yes, I feel much better now. A person shouldn't bottle up emotions. It doesn't do a person any good. (*A deep breath*) Okay ... we're back now, Newton. Back on Main Street. Bring on the clowns and the funny stuff. (*Excitedly*) Oh, oh, oh, Newton, look-a there, look-a there ... aren't they adorable? I just love those ... those miniature horses. Where do they come from, Newton? They are not of this earth. It's like they're perfect. It's like they're from a special world, Newton. It's like they're real, Newton, real horses, from a world like ours but only perfect and tiny . . . tiny . . . and dot, dot, dot. (*Sighs*) I love a parade.

End of Scene

ODE TO LITTLE AUDREY

Scene

A sidewalk near a city street. Audrey, a young girl (or at least a young girl at heart) is jumping rope. She has all the moves and is quite confident in her rope-jumping ability. Her friend, Newton (although he is not seen), is a novice at jumping rope.

AUDREY: (*Jumping rope and reciting*)
"Tick tock, the game is locked,
Nobody else can play.
And if they do, we'll take their shoe
And we'll beat them black and blue (and purple too!)."

(*She stops jumping*) "Times!" I called "times," Newton. No, no "buttsies!" You cannot call "buttsies" when a person calls "times!" And I called "times," which means everything stops. Your rope, the Earth, even the universe . . . stops! So, "times!" There. That's better. Now stay frozen. I'm going to tie my shoe, Newton, and when I stand up straight, you had better be frozen. (*Bending down to tie shoes*) I would have worn my Velcro tennis shoes today, but my dog chewed 'em up last night. I found them in the yard this morning, and I just laughed because . . . (*laughing*) they aren't my favorite color. Okay, "oxen free!"
(*Resumes jumping and reciting*)

"Tick tock, the game is locked,
Nobody else can play.
And if they do . . ."

(*Stops jumping—showing mild irritation*)
What is the matter with you, Newton? When I say "oxen free," it means you can move. So stand up and get ready to jump. You know, I believe you are walking around in a turkey's

dream! (*Looking down the street*) Hmm. What time is it? Are you sure this is the place? Well, they should be here any minute. Okay, let's practice a double Dutch. Here we go . . . (*Jumping*)

"I like coffee, I like tea.
I like Newton to jump with me!
One, two, three, four, five . . ."

(*She stops*)

Newton, are you going to jump in? Double Dutch, Newton, jump with me! Get ready, now; you can't be sloppy and double Dutch . . . you've got to be right on time. (*Stops*) What is it? (*Studies the approaching caravan of cars*) Oh . . . here they come. And look, they all have their headlights on, Newton, and the policeman is waving them through the stop sign. Which car is she in? The first or the second? (*Nodding*) First. And your family is in the second. Hmmm. (*Matter-of-factly*) You know, Newton, my grandpa was killed by a train a few years ago. He was. And I saw it happen, but I've never talked about it much. You see, Grandpa and I had been to Barkley's Horse and Feed Store and we were walking back to town, when Grandpa saw a silver dollar on the train tracks in the distance . . . and he ran off after it. Grandpa couldn't hear very well, and well, when he bent down to pick up the coin, this old train smacked Grandpa . . . like a bug on a windshield . . . and . . . I . . . just . . . laughed . . . knew all along it was just a nickel. That's right, Newton. (*Laughing*) It was just a nickel. (*Noticing*) The car has stopped, Newton, and I guess it's time to jump to Grandma's rhyme. Ready. Here we go. (*Jumping rope*)

"Down in the valley
Where the green grass grow
There sat Grandma

Sweet as a rose
She sang, she sang,
She sang so sweet;
Along came Grandpa
And kissed her on the cheek.
How many kisses did she get that day?

One, two, three, four . . ."

(*They stop skipping and watch the car pass by. Audrey begins to laugh*)
You know, Newton, your Grandmother was a pretty good rope-jumper, too, until she broke her hip. But you must get your talent for jumping rope from your Grandfather's side of the family, because you jump rope like a rooster in mud. (*Skipping off and reciting*)

"Charlie Chaplin went to France
To teach the ladies how to dance;
First the heel and then the toe,
A skip and a hop and away you go!"

End of Scene

HUMMERS, ROCKETS, AND SPLIT COMETS

Scene

A clear summer night on the Fourth of July. Shelley (a girl in her mid- to late teens) reaches a landing on the rugged hillside to watch the city fireworks display. She lays out a blanket, takes in the night air, marvels at the view, and calls out to her boyfriend, Newton, who is having trouble climbing the hill to reach her.

SHELLEY: (*Excited and lifting her hands skyward*) There it is. Just waiting for someone to paint it, like a backdrop, a canvas primed and stretched tight. What a beautiful night! So bright and promising. (*Calling down to Newton*)

Come on, Newton, hurry up! You're going to miss the finale! And, if you miss it, all bets are off! (*Delighting in the sights and sounds*) I love those hummers, rockets, and split comets. None of that "egg-laying hen" stuff you were passing off as fireworks in your backyard, Newton. (*Inhaling*) This is the real *pa-boom*! Sky monkeys loaded with ladyfingers! Flowering chrysanthemums! (*She imitates the sound of fireworks*) *Pa-boom. Pop! Pop! Pop! Pop! Pa-boom!* (*Pleasantly startled*) Wow! Did you see that? Hurry, Newton, this place is perfect! It's like we have the July sky all to ourselves. No one else around. Just you and me . . . and this blanket . . . and me . . . and the bright, beautiful night sky. Just like in the movies . . . it's perfect!

(*Reciting her Latin*)

"*Mica, mica, parva stella*
Miror, quaenam si tam bella!"

(*To Newton*) It's Latin for . . .

"Twinkle, twinkle, little star
How I wonder what you are."

Some people say Latin is a dead language, Newton. I think it's romantic. *"Mica, mica, parva stella,"* and it has great dignity. (*Echoing the fireworks*) Pa-boom! Like these magnificent fireworks, Latin is one of the great accomplishments of the entire world. Mr. Halley, my science teacher, said I should study Latin if I plan to go into medicine, which I do, or, chemistry, because I just love mixing chemicals, and making fireworks, Newton. A little potassium nitrate and a pinch of sulfur just about sends me to the moon. Who knows, maybe I'll be a fireworks artist and governors and prime ministers and presidents from all around the world will employ me to create their shows.

(*Echoing the sound*) Pa-boom. Did you see that? *Pop! Pop! Pop! Pop!* It will be over soon, Newton. I told you not to wear those flip-flops. I warned you, Newton. I said you wouldn't be able to climb to the top in those. I told you. (*Echoing*) *Ka-boom! Ka-boom!* That was more beautiful than all the *parva stellas* in the sky. It was perfect! Hurry, Newton! The finale is almost here! And I want it to be just like that old movie we watched. You, Newton, will be Cary Grant and, I, Shelley, will be Grace Kelly, and the fireworks will be the fireworks except these will be in color and more spectacular, so pull yourself up here, Newton! And don't, for Christ's sake, fall! It's a long, long way down.

(*Echoing*) *Ka-boom!* Did you see that?! Of course not. You have your face against the wall. (*With great excitement*) That was incredible! Oh, wow! It was like a blooming white flower filling the sky. And when it seemed like it was over, and the last of the petals began to fade, green frogs began leaping in all directions, landing on the bellies of surprised water snakes, who, spitting and fizzing, whipped about, flinging sparks, helter-skelter into the night sky. It was amazing, Newton. And I want it to happen again and again! *Ka-boom! Ka-boom! Ka-boom!* Hurry, Newton, it's the finale! *Ka-boom!* *"Mica, mica, parva stella!"* I just want to reach up and grab this wonderful night! (*Reaching upward*) Or maybe you, Newton. My Cary Grant, hurry! On a night light this, with a sky like that, anything is possible. That's right, Newton, anything! (*Silence. She listens*)

Well. Hmmm . . . I guess that's it. I guess it's over. (*Drawing in a breath and then exhaling*) Ahhh . . . well . . . I guess you missed the finale, Newton. It certainly was a beautiful sight. (*Sighs, nonchalantly*) Well, who knows, maybe you will make it next year. I'm coming down, Newton. I'm coming down.

End of Scene

F = Wᴅ

Scene

A college dorm room. Sarah, an intense student, anxious about an upcoming exam, has had a confrontation with another student on her floor. Sarah storms into her dorm room, venting her anger to a nonresponsive roommate.

SARAH: (*Shouting back down the hall*) Kiss my butt! (*Stepping into her room*) That girl drives me crazy! She thinks I'm trying to steal her boyfriend . . . Newton. Newton! (*To her roommate*) You've seen him, Ruthie. He's living proof that we were not made in God's image! (*Stomping about*) Ohh. I'm not in the mood for this! I'm feeling really shaky, Ruthie, unbalanced. I've got a calculus exam tomorrow and a rash on my butt from sitting all day in a metal chair! (*Trying to get Ruthie's attention*)

Did you hear what happened out there, Ruthie? All I did was knock on Newton's door and ask if I could borrow a pencil . . . to do my math . . . and then his girlfriend . . . the frigging Frog Lady . . . leaps out into the hall and croaks, "I know what you're thinking!" And so I yell back, "You do? Okay, tell me: When does the formula $F = Wd$ not apply?" To which she answered, "His pencil!" Jesus, Ruthie, psych majors! They see the whole world through Freudian sunglasses . . . or maybe she's got some Victorian novel stuck up her ass. I don't know. But I do know . . . I've had it up to here with the fruitcakes on this floor . . . the conjoined snickering Darby twins . . . Danny android and his computer perversity, and that slimy nose-picker next door. I'm sick of all of them! And especially the Frog Lady, so I took off on her, Ruthie. And I make no apologies. "You're wrong, Frog Lady! (*Building up steam*) Think about the formula this way. You are a *constant force* to deal with . . . see . . . so Frog Lady equals F, which stands for *force*. Now you weigh, I'd say, in that neighborhood of about . . . one hundred and sixty pounds, more or more. And you're trying your damnedest to throw your saturated beef around, see, pushing me just ten feet down the hall . . . here. So, in this example the work done is ten times one hundred sixty, or 1,600 foot-pounds. But! But! Here's the real answer to my question, Frog Lady. If you are knocked on your ass . . . say . . . by an irate, sleep-deprived science major . . . me . . . before you push her . . . me . . . ten feet, the formula $W = Fd$ does not apply!"

Well, Ruthie, I think that was an educated response, don't you? I mean, suddenly, I found some real application of the study of differential calculus. Well, the Frog Lady was stunned like she'd been hit by an air gun. I waited for a response . . . something well timed, studious, enlightened. Then, Ruthie, get this! She stuck out her tongue. (*Demonstrating*) Like this. And suddenly I saw Amanda Fleming from my third-grade class . . . and I knew, I knew the perfect response. "No, thank you. I use toilet paper." How about that for expanding the boundaries of knowledge? Do I really need a diploma?

We are doomed, Ruthie. Ruthie? (*Studies Ruthie*) Are you listening to me? You didn't hear a word I said, did you? You have your earplugs in again, don't you?! For crying out loud and lonely, Ruthie, turn off that *Papa Loves Mambo* crap and listen to me. I'm talking education here, Ruthie. Higher education. Wait a minute. Here's a thought. Fifth grade, little Kathy Taylor, the boys followed her like they were drugged.
(*She yells down the hallway*)

If you don't like my apples,
Then don't shake my tree;
I'm not after your boyfriend,
He's after me!

Ha! (*Feeling pleased with herself*) You know, Ruthie, this is kind of fun. Therapeutic. Yeah. I'm feeling much better. I think I'll cancel my appointment with the mental health center. Do you want to order a pizza?

End of Scene

STAGE FRIGHT PIANOLOGUE

Scene

A recital hall. A piano, off center, rests on the stage. The instrument is there to be used by an accompanist for a light opera audition about to take place. The accompanist, Nicole, enters hurriedly from the wings. She takes a moment to study the piano and the surroundings, then seeks out the music director seated in the auditorium. Nicole's stutter is a result of extreme nervousness and a few phobias.

NICOLE: (*Wringing her hands*) Are you th . . . th . . . the music director? I was told I'd find you in here. I'm . . . ah . . . the piano. I mean . . . I . . . ah . . . I play the piano. I'm ah . . . I'm ah . . . the accompanist. I was told to be here at two . . . to . . . to . . . relieve the other pianist. (*Checking a wristwatch that isn't there*) Am I late? No. Good. So you're taking a break . . . now . . . oh, okay . . . so I . . . ah . . . have some time . . . ah . . . to organize . . . review . . . the music . . . and . . . ah . . . get ready . . . for the singers. (*Makes her way to the piano*) Okay. Well . . . I'm sorry if I seem a little shaky. I'm a beginner. I've worked with singers in practice rooms but not in public. So I'm just a little bit nervous, I'm afraid, standing . . . here . . . here . . . on the . . . on the . . . ah . . . stage. (*Beginning to shake*) I have a . . . have a . . . ah . . . little stage fright . . . theatrophobia . . . according to my doctor . . . Dr. Newton. (*Nervous laughter*) Hehehe! But . . . ah . . . but . . . ah . . . but . . . I'll be all right. Whew! It's freezing in here! Boy, are my hands cold. (*Clapping her hands, wriggling and talking to her fingers*) Okay, fellows, take off your warm-up pants and put on your dancing shoes . . . it's time to tap the ivories. (*She laughs*) Hehehehe.

Say . . . how many . . . how many . . . how many people does this theater seat? Ohhh. (*Overwhelmed*) About four . . . four . . . four hundred. Wow! Whew! Okay . . . and the singers are auditioning for light operas . . . American musicals . . . and . . . ahh . . . Gilbert and Sullivan . . . right? (*Trying to be positive*) Ohh . . . good . . . some of my favorites . . . (*Failing*) well, not really . . . sometimes all that bantering . . . all that wordplay . . . you know . . . makes me a little nervous. (*Fearfully*) They're not going to recite poetry, are they? Oh, great. It's just that Dr. Newton thinks I have a little fear of poetry. . . . Metrophobia . . . with a just a . . . a . . . you know, a slight touch of . . . a . . . verbaphobia . . . a fear . . . of . . . of . . . words . . . but . . . I'll be fine as long as you don't ask me to recite anything. Breathe! (*She does*) Wow! That was a dry mouthful. (*She laughs*) Hehehehe.

I feel better now. (*Changing the subject—again, trying to be optimistic*) So . . . how's your mother? Oh . . . (*Stunned*) she's not alive? I'm . . . I'm . . . ah . . . sorry. Dr. Newton told me that one of the best ways to overcome stage fright is to pretend I'm chatting to a friend. That's why I asked . . . about . . . your . . . well . . . forgive me.

Oh, what do you know? (*Wriggling her fingers*) I think they are getting warm. (*She laughs*) Hehehehe. (*Checking the music and the names of those auditioning*)

Okay . . . let me see . . . now . . . here's the music for the next few auditions. (*Talking to herself*) "Hey, what do you know, Nicole?" Oh, that's my name, by the way. You can call me . . . ahh . . . Nicky. Okay. "You know all these singers . . . they're in your music classes . . . and you love them and you really want to help them succeed today." Dr. Newton . . . said . . . that I should think . . . just positive thoughts. (*Begins to shake*) "This is sure going to be a lot of fun, Nicky." (*Nervous laughter—on the verge of exploding*) Hehehehe.

You know, this is a big room. Whew! (*Mounting anxiety*) It's high and wide and deep . . . and . . . and I think I'm fine with it . . . except my throat is tightening . . . just a . . . just a . . . little. Nothing really. I mean that last session with Dr. Newton in that abandoned warehouse . . . ah . . . basically . . . ah . . .

purged my fear of kenophobia . . . large, empty spaces. But this isn't really an empty space . . . it's a theater . . . hehehehe . . . which . . . I believe I told you . . . makes me a little bit nervous . . . nauseous . . . maybe it's because the theater contains all of my fears: theatro, glosso, halo, keno, metro, verba . . . and probably the worst . . . being stared at . . . opthalmophobia . . . like right now . . . by you! (*Her anxiety peaks—almost hysterical*) But don't, don't . . . be afraid . . . because it's okay. You see . . . I'm not afraid . . . because . . . I am . . . I am . . . not really a pianist. No. (*Shedding all fears*) I'm an actor. (*In control* . . .) The child of Thespis. The craftsman of Dionysus. Vocal. Physical. Beautiful. Emo . . . emo . . . emotional. (. . . *but not for long*) Wow! And you are wearing . . . ah . . . yellow boxers! I'm . . . I'm . . . sorry. I'm supposed to imagine you in your underwear. It is hot in here. Very hot. I can't breathe. Nauseous. Very nauseous. And I need a drink of water. I've got to go . . . get some . . . (*A speedy exit*)

End of Scene

Chapter 4

BUCKAROO BELLE AND
THE BULL RIDER

Scene

A rodeo. Katie Belle, a young bull-riding instructor, coaches Newton, a newcomer to the sport of competitive bull riding. Katie Belle's excitement and knowledge of the sport shine through as she helps Newton prepare for his ride.

KATIE BELLE: (*Excitedly*) Just eight seconds, Newton. Yee-hahh! Just eight tiny ticks of the clock, and it's all over, boy. You'll walk away with one thousand big ones in the back pocket of those new dungarees. But the best part, Newton, you'll be holdin' up those jeans with a shining new belt buckle . . . diamond studded, with your name branded in the leather! You can't beat that, boy! You've just got to hang on for eight seconds!

(*Watching a rider*) Look-a there. Gates open! (*Cheering*) Ride 'em, cowboy. Bam! (*The bull tosses the rider*) Whew! That was quick! (*To Newton—amazed*) Did you see that?! It was all humping and horns. That bull bucked so hard he almost took that cowboy's head off! Mercy! That is one buckin' bull. That rider didn't even bounce. Whoo-ee! And he almost lost that foot race to the fence! Yes sirree! That bull almost reamed him out! Wow! Now, that's action! That's entertainment. (*Calling out*) I wanna ride that bull some day. Sign me up, foreman!

Okay, Newton, maybe we should practice a little bit. (*Moving toward an exercise barrel*) We're gonna do a warm-up exercise. You gotta be in the proper frame of mind to beat the bull, Newton. So climb up there on that barrel. We're going to visualize the ride. We'll go through all the motions and imagine each move. I'll ride alongside you. (*Mounting a barrel*) You know, Newton, I've been teaching cowboys to ride since I was eight. (*Proudly*) My daddy taught me. I don't mean to brag, but I helped him coach three Junior Regional

Champions. And I think I'm gonna get a rodeo scholarship to Jackson Community College. (*A brief moment of reflection*) I don't know. I'd like to make a living at this . . . riding the circuit . . . there's big money . . . but I'm also considering other vocations. I might be an artist or a physicist or maybe I'll work for the FBI. I have a hard head . . . and I think it takes a hard head to do any of those things well. But I don't have to decide for a while . . . and so right now . . . I just love riding these bulls.

(*Confidentially*) I'm gonna tell you a secret my daddy told me, Newton. It's all about the bull's motion—finding his rhythm and adjusting yours. That's just plain old physics! Now the art of bull riding has to do with . . . ease . . . and you have to make it look beautiful . . . like a dance. And finally, you've got to ask yourself just one question before they open the gate: Are your balls bigger than the bull's? Because if they ain't, you're in the wrong place.

(*Getting down to business*) Now you'll be riding Starburst, Newton. He's a five-year-old and he's bucked fifteen riders, but I think he's ready to give up the eight seconds to the right man. I think you're the one. But first, Newton, I want you to visualize a perfect ride in slow motion up here on these barrels. Here we go. Just relax. Good. Smell the bull. (*She takes a deep breath*) Hmm . . . he smells good, don't he? (*Going through the motions*) Now, grip the leather rope in your hand and lift your free hand way back—ready to slice the air. Easy does it. Relaxed and balanced, just sittin' on top of old Starburst, we're gonna take a little ride around the world. It feels goooood up here. Now, breathe deep one last breath; I want you to imagine something beautiful, like biscuits and butter, or maybe me, Katie Belle. Once that vision is planted in your head, I'll give the word, the chute gate will open, and you will . . . (*Distracted by a rider*) Hey, look-a there, Newton. It's your friend. Ol' Hurley. He's riding Diablo. That bull is one mean six-year-old! (*Calling out*) Go get him, Hurley!

(*To Newton*) He's quick . . . just watch how he explodes out of the chute. He'll make a couple jumps, and then there's a ninety percent chance he'll spin, like a whirl-a-gig, to the right. (*Cheering*) Go get him, Hurley. (*Broadcasting*) Gates opened. Whoa! There he goes! Hang on, Hurley! Hang on! He's in trouble! Don't panic! He's going to his left, Hurley! Watch it! Wow! (*The rider is tossed*) Lift off! He's flying! All four feet off the ground! Get out of there, Hurley! That was some ride! (*With great fanfare*) Yee-hahh! That bull exploded! I mean, just three seconds in . . . Diablo came to a complete stop . . . then he launched into the air just like a rocket! Like he was defying gravity! And Ol' Hurley . . . was just tossed on his head . . . like he was nothing! Now, that was excitement. That was a ride!

(*She turns to Newton*) Did you see that, Newton? (*He is gone*) Newton? Now, where did he go? Newton. Hmmm. Maybe he went after a helmet. (*Calling out*) Hey, foreman, I want to ride old Diablo. Sign me up!

End of Scene

CHOCOLATE THIN MINTS

Scene

A college administration office. Virginia, a first-year college student, slightly overweight, enters the office of Mr. Newton, Director of Residential Life. Virginia's quick Southern speech and overt personality overwhelm Mr. Newton.

VIRGINIA DARE: (*Forcefully*) Hey. Are you Mr. Newton? Good. I was told I needed to talk to you about roommate assignments? Mine isn't working out. Irreconcilable differences. It's time for a divorce.

My name is Virginia. Virginia Dare . . . just like the first-born child in the New World. (*Making sure he understands*) My roommate's name is Lilith Cain. We've been roommates now for almost a whole semester. I didn't know Lilith before I came to school here. She's from the North and I'm from the South . . . and, well . . . I was naturally just a tad apprehensive; I'd never spent much time in the North. Just one weekend in the Big Apple. The Greenville Flappers, an elite group of highly dedicated high-school flag-twirlers, which, I might add, are still my best friends, performed in the St. Patrick's Day Parade. I love New York. So it's not like I'm fighting the Civil War. (*A quick breath*) And don't get me wrong, I love this school and I want to honor that part in our preamble that states: "Each student is a bright piece of glass in our cultural mosaic." I appreciate that. (*Sincerely*) I do. It's just that, I don't understand her speech, Mr. Newton, and that's a problem because she talks nonstop.

(*A quick breath*) Another thing, between you and me, I think she's too skinny. (*Feigning confidentiality*) And I don't want to spread rumors, and I so hope that I'm wrong, but she might be bulimic. Lord have mercy. (*Amazed*) I mean, she eats a lot, but I don't know where it goes. She has a full meal plan, one of those compact refrigerators stuffed with bagels and cream cheese, and the top drawer of her dresser is layered with boxes of Girl Scout cookies. They say that sharks will eat anything; well, I swear my roommate is part hammerhead. The way that girl eats, she should weigh more than my Uncle Willie's prize heifer. But, I think she's a size two. That's not much of an exaggeration. (*Knowingly*) I guess it's her metabolism. Or maybe she's just throwing it all up. Whatever, it's not fair.

(*A confession*) I battle my weight constantly. From day one, Lilith has been highly critical of me. You should see the expression on her face if I have just a tiny snack between meals. Well, I'm tired of that! I mean, Mr. Newton, I enrolled in college, not a fat camp.

(*Telling it all*) Last night was the straw that broke the full-figured camel's back. I'm not ashamed to tell you, I woke up about two in the morning, very hungry. (*Setting the scene*) I could smell an open box of those chocolate Thin Mints, my favorite, on top of Lilith's dresser. (*Accusingly*) Sometimes, I swear, she leaves food out just to bait me. Anyway, I couldn't help myself. I took the box . . . the bait . . . crawled back into bed and began to enjoy . . . one after another . . . in total darkness. (*Sensationally*) They were so good. I felt like I was in a delicious dream. (*An awakening*) And then I heard her sharp Yankee voice slicing the quiet of the night: "Virginia, what are you eating?" I had a full cookie in my mouth, and so I pretended not to hear her . . . hoping she'd go back to sleep. A few minutes passed, and then she said: "I know you're awake, Virginia, and it's wrong for someone with your weight problem to be eating cookies in bed in the middle of the night." (*With indignation*) Well, hold me down, who made her my guardian? It was very strange, Mr. Newton, and totally uncalled for. Totally. So I resolved that I would not give up the cookies. (*Recreating the mood—with quiet desperation*) I would be steadfast . . . remain quiet . . . thinking eventually she would go back to sleep. Several minutes passed, and I thought the episode was over. I was about to put another cookie in when suddenly I was hit by a flood of naked light. (*An announcement*) And there she was: Lilith, the Wicked Witch of the North. "I caught you!" she said. "Aren't you ashamed of yourself?" Then she grabbed the box. I started to put up a fight but . . . they were her cookies.

(*A deep breath of exhaustion*) Well, I didn't sleep at all after that, which gave me a lot of time to come to this conclusion: I don't want a skinny roommate any longer. (*Decisively*) So, Mr. Newton, we need to check your files for a few good candidates. And I'm going to interview them this time until I find a good match. (*A discovery*) Say, are those Fig Newtons in that jar? Well of course they are, ding-a-ling! (*Self-mockingly*) Mr. Newton. Those are my favorite. Do you mind?

End of Scene

Chapter 4

THE TWILIGHT ARCH

Scene
An open field. The night sky is clear and filled with stars. Two young college students, Torrie and Newton, have climbed a ridge to take in the landscape and to listen for the howling of coyotes.

TORRIE: This is the spot. This is the best place in the county to hear them. (*Sitting*) I know some kids go over to Reuben's Ridge, but I like this place, this hill. (*Removing her shoes*) It's like a natural outdoor theater or something. I'm taking off my shoes, Newt. (*Wriggling her toes*) I'm planting my toes in the earth to see if they take root. That feels right, Newt. Take off yours. And look at the stars. How bright! How they light up the sky! Professor Andersen has a bumper sticker on his truck. Have you seen it? It's crazy, Newt, it says, "Light speed. 185,000 miles per second. It's the law." He's a character. (*She laughs*) He makes me laugh. I'm getting excited. They will start soon, Newt. Soon. (*Slight pause—inquisitively*)

Why don't you talk, Newt? Don't you have anything to say? I know you're real smart. You do well on all the exams. But you don't talk. The kids were saying the other day that no one has even heard the sound of your voice. What is it, Newt? Don't you want to be heard? Don't you want others to hear what you have to say? You know, thoughts are just words in your head . . . but if you let them out . . . and you add just a little sound . . . they become music. I didn't make that up. It's what my mom always says. But she also says, "There is good music and there is bad music." (*She rises*)

Look, Newton. (*Pointing*) There it is. Just like the professor told us. What did he call it, Newt? You remember. The arch. Yes, the twilight arch—you see, there, a pink band of color in the sky with the dark area underneath. What did he say? (*Recalling*) It's the Earth casting its shadow on our atmosphere. You see it, don't you Newt? It's amazing! And a little bit ominous. We are so lucky to be here. Under the sky. With our toes in the earth. (*She rises*) They will start soon. Oh, I love to hear them. Sometimes, when I'm bored or trapped by school or home or friends, I think of the coyotes . . . out here . . . roaming the land . . . free . . . and howling. The sound digs deep, Newt, and it makes me feel good, right here inside, to hear the cry of the coyotes. They make me smile. Look, I've made you smile. (*Again, sitting beside Newton*) Your eyes are very expressive.

You know, Newt, I feel like I can trust you . . . with a secret . . . and it's not because you don't talk. It's because your eyes are very honest. And I want to be honest, too. (*Pause*) Last summer. It was unreal. Chaotic. I didn't think it could happen to me. (*Innocently*) I thought I was protected, but I guess I wasn't. It was the first time I had had a long-term relationship. (*Emotions bubble up*) The first time I cared about someone so deeply. But we were too young. Too afraid. And so, we made the decision. Drove to a clinic. Filled out the paperwork. Answered questions. Were given instructions about how to prevent it from happening again. Then . . . they took it. And it was over. (*Sight pause*) I wanted to hide. At first I felt very emotional . . . and then . . . empty. I thought I was protected. I thought . . . it wouldn't happen to me. (*Slight pause—a deep breath*) And I thought . . . if I told someone else . . . you, Newton . . . if I put it into words . . . I wouldn't have these thoughts anymore. (*Trying to brush the feelings away*) Mother would say, it's bad music. (*Rises*)

Let me see if I can think of something good. (*Locating her smile*) What about . . . (*Looking at the sky*) celestial mechanics? Isn't that what the professor wrote on the board today? Celestial mechanics. I don't know what it means, but I like the sound. (*The coyotes howl*) Shhh. There. Listen. (*Excitedly*) They are howling, Newton. Howling. Isn't it beautiful? Isn't it the most beautiful sound you've ever heard? (*A forceful whisper*) Aaaoooohh! Aaaoooohh!! Come on, Newton, we should join in their song. (*She begins to howl*) Aaaoooohh! Aaaoooohh! (*Encouraging*) Howl, Newton, howl. It will make you laugh.

End of Scene

LIZZIE'S LILLIPUT

Scene

A campus mall area. Lizzie, a young student, watches a group of kids engaged in mock medieval battles using Nerf toys. Her friend and participating warrior, Newton, completes a round of the battle game and collapses on the ground near her.

LIZZIE: (*To Newton*) Whoa! (*Referring to the last attack on Newton*) That was quite the wallop! Are you taking a break now, Newton? Good. Because you must be exhausted running around like that. (*Shaking her head*) I don't know, Newton. I'd like to join some clubs . . . I mean, being new here at the school and all . . . but pretending to dress like a refugee from King Arthur's Court and beating other students with Nerf swords isn't what I had in mind. (*Trying to be nice*) It kind of looks like fun . . . but it also seems . . . well . . . childish. I guess I'm thinking of joining clubs with more of a social agenda . . . But don't get me wrong, Newton, I like you and I don't want you to think I'm a stick-in-the-mud.

(*With a slight degree of self-importance*) I didn't always behave this way, this grown-up, this mature, Newton. For a while I was a bleached blond boxie, a glitterbag, and then a bizotic, i.e., bizarre plus exotic equals weird, and then finally, a brainiac. As you might guess, there were many bumps in the road on the way to finding my intelligence, Newton. I used to talk like, "Duh," "You know," "I mean," like a Val girl, and then one day my speech teacher, Mr. Bell, dropped a bomb in class. Ka-boom! He quoted Jonathan Swift, the guy who wrote *Gulliver's Travels*, who said, ". . . every word we speak is in some degree a diminution of our lungs by corrosion, and consequently contributes to the shortening of our lives." (*Reliving the shock*) "Oh, God!" I thought. "This is horrible! Why didn't someone tell me before?" You see, throughout my adolescent years, Newton, I was a habitual talker, a blabberer who never shut her mouth. And although I was only fifteen at the time I learned about this talking disease, I figured in terms of the number of words I had spoken in my life, I was probably closer to sixty-five or seventy. And so, I had to quit immediately.

(*A painful memory*) For a whole week I didn't say a word. Not one utterance. It was very painful . . . and it made me really stressed and nervous . . . and at times I could hardly breathe. And let me tell you, all through that week I had uncontrollable urges to talk . . . to say just one word . . . to express . . . or to affirm . . . with just one word. But I stayed strong and resisted. For that whole week, I remained silent. It was very awkward. I didn't know how to explain to my friends that talking was sending me prematurely to the grave, and I didn't want them to think that I had become a "Waldo," and so I wore a sign on my sweater: "I am remaining silent to protest world hunger." It was the most difficult week of my life.

The only thing that saved me was . . . mime. (*Joyfully*) That's right—the ancient art of nonverbal communication. I mimed everything . . . and what I discovered was that I could talk really well with other parts of my body and that everyone seemed to understand everything I said . . . or, I mimed. I was becoming an expert mime . . . and . . . looking in the mirror each day . . . I thought I was getting . . . well . . . younger . . . and beginning to add back all those years I had lost talking my life away. (*A revelation*) Then something dawned on me. Suddenly I could see. My grandmother! My grandmother is ninety-two years old, Newton, and she never shuts up! I mean, she has talked two husbands to death and she is now working on the entire geriatric population at the Happy Valley Retirement Center.

(*Expressed joy*) No, Newton, I realized that talking has not killed her and it will not kill me! Besides, I thought, if this Swift guy was right, then why doesn't the Attorney General warn us with, " . . . talking is hazardous to your health"? That's when I checked out *Gulliver's Travels*. And let me tell you, this Swift guy had quite the imagination . . . and his book isn't even a real travel book; it's a fiction, Newton! This guy Gulliver traveled to bizotic places including the land of the Lilliputians, tiny people no taller than six inches. That's right, Newton, people . . . just six inches tall.

Hey. I have an idea. I'll mime it for you. Imagine if you were Gulliver and I were a Lilliputian . . . and we wanted to take a walk . . . say to get an ice cream cone . . . we couldn't even hold hands because you are like a skyscraper to me. I might be able to reach your shoestring . . . (*She reaches up to grab the imaginary shoestring of Gulliver*) like this . . . but even that would be an enormous stretch. (*Standing on tiptoe*) Like this. (*She walks off on tiptoes with her arm stretched skyward—as if holding on to Gulliver's shoestring*)

End of Scene

TWO BLUSHING PILGRIMS

Scene

A theater. The evening of a dress rehearsal for Romeo and Juliet. *Kari, a costume and makeup assistant, enters from the wings carrying supplies for the evening's rehearsal. She is locked out of the dressing rooms and is looking for Newton, the stage manager, for a key and conversation. A native of Brooklyn, Kari knows that the emotions that run backstage before a performance often surpass the drama on the stage.*

KARI: (*Walking onto the stage and spotting Newton on the catwalk above the seating*) The dressing rooms are locked. I can't get in. Hey, Newton, the dressing rooms are locked. What time was the call? Six thirty? You got a key? I've got more supplies in the car: Streaks 'N Tips, crepe hair, and that block of dry ice for the fog machine. (*Squinting to see Newton*) What is it with your mouth, Newton? Ouch! Looks like you ate a whole cantaloupe or something. Have you been to the dentist today? Ouch! How you gonna call the show if you can't talk? (*Before he can respond*) Ah, what the hell . . . they don't listen to you anyway, right? Just kidding. Come down; I've got something important to ask you. (*Putting down her supplies*) And open the dressing rooms. I've got to make moustaches and bald caps for those pubescent friars . . . and . . . a . . . "But soft! What light through yonder window breaks?" . . . Our chubby little Romeo split his pants again. So, if you've got a key, I've got a sewing needle.

(*Humorously*) Actors. Could they live without me? I doubt it. They need me. I'm like their mother, you know. (*Rattling off issues*) Juliet's having her period; she hates her parents, thinking about getting an apartment. Mercutio told me he's coming out of the closet tonight, before the curtain, at the company meeting. I said, "No, Mercutio, the director wouldn't like that. Save it for the cast party." He tells me, "Kari, I can't wait another minute because I'm sick of living a lie. Besides," he says, "it will free my emotions and liberate my acting." So, stay tuned tonight, Newton; Mercutio will give new meaning to his line: "Here's my fiddlestick; here's that shall make you dance." Thank God, Newton, that theater isn't, in *stricta sensu*, a science. This place would explode like the bull's eye on a test site in Nevada.

(*Building her vision*) The thing is, you've got all this emotion running wild backstage before the show. All this energy. And as each actor arrives and signs his name to the callboard, he tosses more emotion in the mix. (*More rapidly*) So they're all running around looking for me . . . or for anyone who will listen . . . and their heads are popping off, and their pants are ripped, and they are not gay but are gay, and they're pissed off at each other, their mothers, and lovers, and they're crying, and their makeup runs, and their shoes don't fit, and there is not a tampon to be found anywhere! (*She breathes*) It's chaos, Newton. Not one tampon. Theater backstage is human life *in extremis*. (*Sudden pleasantness*) And then, you show up, Newton. Our stage manager. And you say, "Places!" with such authority. And suddenly, they all shut up. Suddenly, there is silence. Suddenly, all that confusion and chaos is gone as they whisper "break a leg" or hug each other, because now there is order, you see; they are working together to make something beautiful . . . or . . . maybe . . . they're just in that state of shock . . . you know, like a deer caught in headlights. (*Smiling*)

Which is the way I felt last night, Newton, with you. Shockingly beautiful . . . and just a little naughty. But, Newton, I don't want you to get the wrong impression. And I don't want to sound like a cliché and say I'm not that kind of girl, because . . . well, I am that kind of girl . . . for you.

(*Enjoying the confession*) And, I just want you to know that you kiss "by the book." And ... well ... if you are free again tonight, and if'n you're not in too much pain with that mouth problem, I want you to know, (*Quoting Romeo*) "My lips, two blushing pilgrims, ready stand ... To smooth that rough touch with a tender kiss." Again and again.

End of Scene

HARD KNOCKS

Scene

A stage. The Firehouse Community Theater is holding audi-
tions for a new production of Annie. *Darcy Wells has been asked*
to help organize all the young, aspiring actors auditioning for
the title role. One by one, she ushers the actors onto the stage and
introduces them to the director, while intermittently talking to
Sandy, the choreographer and musical director.

DARCY WELLS: (*To a child actor*) Smile! That's right. Smile.
Good. Next! (*To the director seated in the theater. Loudly*) Her
number is fourteen! (*To Sandy, who is at the foot of the stage*) It's
in my blood. My grandmother and namesake, Darcy Wells,
attended the Hamilton School of Dramatic Expression in
Lexington. I get my talent from her side of the family. I just
thought there were only horses in Kentucky; I didn't know
they taught drama.

(*To a child actor waiting in the wings*) Okay, next! Center stage
and smile, Angel! Show them your teeth and plenty of 'em.
No, darling, don't start dancing. Stop it! Do you hear? Stop it!
(*Broad announcement*) Now listen up. All of you. That nice lady
right there at the foot of the stage, her name is Sandy, just
like Little Orphan Annie's dog, and Sandy will tell you . . . to
dance . . . and sing . . . when she wants you . . . to dance . . . and
sing. (*Back to the child standing center stage*) Okay, Angel? You can
move back now. Get back in line. (*To all auditioning*) Girls, shhh.
Once again, we are working on body language. Just that. The
director wants to get a good look at you, physically . . . so . . .
shhh . . . this is all nonverbal. Next. Smile! That's good. Keeping
smiling. (*To the director*) Number sixteen.

(*To Sandy*) They insisted that I take this job helping the
director, Sandy, because, and it is not easy for me to say this,
they did not want me to audition. I know it. And I know they
know I know it. (*To a child actor*) Smile! That a girl! Is that

your real hair? (*To the director*) She says it's her real hair. Isn't it cute? (*To the actor*) You can go back now. Next! (*To Sandy*) I was the first Annie to perform at the Firehouse Theater several years ago. Did you see it? Too bad. I have a mid-belty voice, and when I sang, (*singing with some restraint*) "Tomorrow, tomorrow, I love ya, tomorrow. You're only a day away," the audience went wild. But when they revived it the next year, a younger girl replaced me. In just one year, I guess I had gotten too old for the role. Actually, it wasn't my voice, it was my feet. They had grown rather large in a very short period of time . . . and backstage at the auditions . . . I overheard Daddy Warbucks tell the costumer that my tapping sounded more like . . . clogging. (*Showing some pain*) So in just a few months, I went from the title role to one of the mutts in the orphanage. It wasn't fair. Watch your back, Sandy. You cannot trust anyone in show business. Especially Daddy Warbucks. And I thought he was such a great man.

(*To a child actor*) Smile! Step up to the light, honey, lift your chin and smile! "You're never fully dressed without a smile." Good. How much did you pay for the wig? (*Shockingly*) Wait . . . Wait . . . wait a minute! Leapin' lizards! We have an imposter here! A cross-dresser! A charlatan! Bring down the curtain! Take off that wig, you sneaky little rat! (*Dressing him down*) Did you really think you wouldn't be discovered? That you could pass for a girl? Get cast as Annie? I said, take off that wig! You are making a mockery of an American theatrical institution. Little Orphan Annie is every girl's dream, and you should be ashamed for trying to steal her away! Take off that wig, I said! (*The boy removes the wig*)

Well . . . what do you know? (*To the director*) I know this boy! He's my neighbor and he lives on North Whitlock Avenue. (*To Newton*) Okay, Newton, get lost! Vamoose! We're looking for an eleven-year-old girl and not a little river rat— so scram! If we do a production of *Oliver*, we'll call you. So, hit the road, Romeo. (*Stunned by a suggestion from the director*)

What? What did you say? You're going to give him an audition? As Annie?!!! Well . . . okay . . . well . . . you're the director. (*To Newton*) All right. Back in line, Newton. I said, back in line! Okay. Next! Eighteen.

(*To Sandy*) Well, Sandy . . . can you believe that man? You know, this is the problem with theater in America . . . directors! Directors with their funny ideas. Doesn't that beat all? Casting a boy as Annie. Well . . . I can see the reviews now: "The sun will come out tomorrow . . . in drag! Surprise! A must-see! This Little Orphan has balls!" Hmmm . . . well, it's the theater . . . and it's a hard-knock life. Hmmm . . . I wonder if he would let me audition for Daddy Warbucks? Just an idea. Next! Smile!

End of Scene

Head Shots and Hot Buttered Biscuits

Scene

An empty stage. Charlotta, although she has worldly experience and some age, is a relative newcomer to the stage. As she walks to the edge of the stage, her extreme makeup and flamboyant dress become apparent; as she speaks, her Southern dialect emerges. Charlotta has asked a director of a nearby community theater to help her prepare to audition.

CHARLOTTA: (*Addressing Ludwig, a director, seated in the auditorium*) What do you think of my head shot? (*Holding up her résumé*) Do I need a new eight-by-ten? (*Projecting her voice*) Can you hear me all right, Ludwig? Are you listening? Do you mind if I call you by your first name, Ludwig? You can just nod. Good.

(*Parroting*) You've got to have a great photo in this business. It's, like, the first thing they see, you know, unless, of course, you know someone, and then it doesn't matter. You can hand them a stick drawing or a Wal-Mart photo print and it works. (*She gasps*) But I don't know anyone in the business. Well, except you, Ludwig. And . . . uh . . . you're not exactly Oprah Winfrey, now are you? Just kidding about that. (*Flatteringly*) I know you're good. I saw that production you directed downtown at the Firehouse Theater and I figure if you could direct that idiot Darcy Wells and make her look like she had half a brain, you could help me with my audition pieces.

(*She gasps*) I just think it might be too glossy, you know what I mean? I asked the photographer, Newton was his name, to touch up that scar over my right eye, but he said no, it gives me character, you know, like Marilyn Monroe's mole. I said, "I don't want character; I want beauty." But he got the last word because he's the professional, even though he looks like he's about ten years old. (*Highlighting*) Newton's Studio: Photographer of the Stars. Barf! (*Suspiciously*) He claims he photographs fashion models . . . and I was thinking Tyra Banks, but it turned out to be Wal-Mart employees and their chubby little children. (*Shaking her head*) You know what I'm talking about? You've seen their circulars, haven't you? "Here's Tasha. Her dad works in Customer Service." And now I'm stuck with fifty of these eight-by-tens. Ouch!

Well, hell's bells, but if you can keep a secret (*Ensuring their privacy*), I might have a little P.S.—(*Whispering*) plastic surgery—to remove that scar before I start a film career, which I plan to do . . . any day now. And maybe while I'm at it . . . I'll tighten up the booty. But I'm not real comfortable with that idea just yet because just yesterday I read about this lady, I think she was a fashion model too, who asked her surgeon to add shape to her butt . . . which I guess they can do now, Ludwig. Anyway, it seems he used those silicone breast implants, planted one in each cheek, and now . . . ouch . . . she's got boobs on her butt! Let me repeat that: boobs on her butt! She's sporting two pair: one upstairs and one on her derrière. I imagine she's just a little bit angry and her boyfriend is a little bit overwhelmed. So, I'm thinking, I'll wait awhile on the butt surgery. It's not too bad, is it? My butt? (*Catching his eye and delighting in his embarrassment*) Ludwig, I believe you are turning red. Yes. Well, what do you know? You are blushing! I believe I have embarrassed you, child, talking about my body parts. I must have stimulated your little red head. Who would have guessed? A worldly man like you . . . a man of the theater . . . a man who has seen or at least imagined it all . . . would turn that shade of red so easily. (*Laughing*) Forgive me. I don't mean to laugh. Please.

(*Drawing breath*) Now, back to business. Did you look at the ... backside ... of my résumé, Ludwig? (*Turning her résumé over*) Hmmm ... I had some trouble with this. You see, I didn't know how much information to include. I want them to know that I'm not a beginner. Right? (*Proud of her accomplishments*) And as you can see, for two whole years ... I was the Decapitated Princess, Stella, in Dr. Magic's Show of Optical Tricks. It was called the "Tavern of the Dead," and it was a lot of fun until Dr. Magic decided to expand his act to include sword swallowing and knife throwing. (*Feigning fear*) Well, the last thing I need are multiple scars, and so it was time for me to resign.

And there, at the bottom of the page, someone told me to list my special skills, which, I admit, are limited, and so, as you can see, I've included Hula-Hoop trickster and horseback rider. (*Seeking reassurance*) Well, I am an expert Hula-Hooper, but between you and me, I've never been on a horse. I did ride an elephant for a whole season with Winky's Little Top Circus and it was a lot of fun, but I believe all that jostling caused me to have irregular periods, and I lost all interest in dating. But I didn't fall off, and so I figured, if I can ride one four-legged beast, I could wrap my legs around any of them. Whoops! (*Suppressing laughter*) That didn't sound very nice, did it? If you don't shut me up, I'll talk until doomsday, and I just might say something I'll regret ... and embarrass us both. So, on with the show. (*She takes a deep breath, walks a few steps to center stage, and begins her audition*)

My name ... oh ... I was told I should first announce my name and then announce the piece. (*Seeking confirmation*) Is that right, Ludwig? Just nod your head. Okay, so, here goes. (*Breathing deeply*) My name is Charlotta Corday (*Whispering*), that's my stage name, by the way (*Resuming full voice*), and for my first audition, I am doing Maggie from *Cat on a Hot Tin Roof* by Tennessee Williams. (*A forceful announcement*) "One of those no-neck monsters hit me with a hot buttered biscuit, so I have t' change!" (*She tries to hold her laughter but fails*) Oh, God, Ludwig. I can hardly say that without laughing. (*Stepping toward Ludwig*) Do you know this play? It is soooo good. You have a nice smile, Ludwig. Are you gay?

End of Scene

Chapter 4

BEAST BALLET

Scene

A dance rehearsal room. The ballet "Beauty and the Beast" is in rehearsal on a stage adjacent to the rehearsal room. Renee, a young, energetic, and overly confident prima ballerina, is working with the inexperienced Newton, a newly recruited member of the company.

RENEE: (*Assuming the proper ballet position as she demonstrates and instructs Newton*) First position. Heels together. Good. Feet turned out. More. More. Ouch, I know it hurts, Newton, but in first position you have to make a single line with your feet. Okay? Out, left foot, out, right foot. Yuck! (*She breaks from the position. Showing slight disdain*) You know Newton, you have a bad case of knock-knee . . . I mean, honestly, it's a physical defect . . . and it looks extremely unpleasant on a dancer . . . unless you join a company of orangutans . . . but don't cry about it. Who knows, in a year or two, if you stay in ballet, you just might grow out of it. I did. (*Again, assumes first position*)

Okay, now, *entrechat!* (*She gestures with her arms but stops before the leap and laughs*) Just kidding. You're not ready for that yet! We'll concentrate on the five positions . . . only . . . so that we can plant you in the *corps* . . . in the forest scene. (*A joyous prediction*) This, Newton, is going to be the greatest production of *Beauty and the Beast* ever. (*Feeling good*) Ouch. John, our choreographer, danced with the Royal Danish Ballet when they visited Tallahassee last fall. Yes! He's good! But we need more bodies, trees, that's all, nothing special.

(*Instructing*) Second position. Open it up. Keep the feet out. Out, out, I say! Balance . . . good . . . good . . . hold it! (*Stepping around Newton*) Now, I'm going to step in front of you, Newton, if I can move around your knees—just kidding—(*Executing the move*) and I'll make the fourth position *efface*, like this, while you stay in second. See. Now we're making a tree for the forest. See. There. Nothing to it. Now put your hands around my waist. Good, good . . . Good God, Newton! (*Showing disgust*) Look at the hair on the back of your hands. Yuck! I've never seen so much hair on a person's hands before. Look how thick it is, and black! You know, I don't like hair on a man. But if you have to grow it, you could at least keep it under your shirt. Ha! Just kidding. But not really. You must still be evolving.

Okay. (*Again, instructing and executing the move*) Third position. Return to first . . . well . . . now each heel touches the middle of the opposite foot. Right. (*Feeling good*) Ouch. Feels good, doesn't it? Hold it, hold it, balance, breathe. You are going to be one stumpy tree, Newton, with your short, knotty legs and very long torso. (*Enjoying this a little too much*) But you can't do a thing about a structural defect like that . . . unless you start to grow . . . so . . . sorry to be the messenger . . . but you won't be doing a solo any time soon. Oh, but don't you love the third position . . . it just pushes everything up . . . doesn't it? (*Breathing deep and standing tall*) Can you feel it, Newton? It forces you to think strong. In control. I feel like I'm on a launch pad, like I am a powerful whirligig, Newton, about to conquer space. I wish we could stay in this position forever. Ouch! How many times have you heard that, Newton? Whoops . . . not very often I bet! But don't cry about it; we must move on.

(*Instructing*) Fourth position. Right foot out, toe and heel line up . . . and good. (*Slight pause*) You know, it must be this production, but just last night I dreamed that a monster, an ogre who was trying to eat me, was chasing me. It was horrible, Newton. (*Reliving the emotions of the dream*) The monster was filthy . . . and hairy . . . and my heart was pounding . . . and terror was taking over . . . as I ran through a dark forest . . . trying desperately to escape. But it became increasingly clear that I could not outrun him! (*Stepping out of position*) Oh, God! His putrid smell and hot breath burned the back of my neck, and I knew I was about to take my last . . . when suddenly . . . I tripped over a tree stump! Ouch! Oh, God! And when I rolled over . . . and opened my eyes to the monster . . . yuck! Guess what?!! (*She laughs*) It was I. The monster was me, Newton! Ha! I was so relieved . . . that I gave myself a kiss . . . and then the two of us did this lovely *pas de deux* as we danced out of the forest. I woke up thinking I've been working too hard.

But ballet is worth it . . . and to be the best . . . it must be beautiful . . . and to be beautiful . . . you must make the unnatural seem natural . . . and so . . . fifth position. (*Demonstrating*) Box the feet, Newton. Good . . . good. You know, Newton, you're not nearly as awkward as you look . . . (*Studies his appearance*) and you are not totally unattractive. But you might see a doctor about that hand hair . . . or at least try combing it. So, that's the lesson. Time to go. Go, Newton, go rehearse with the others. Be a beautiful tree. But wait. Wait. You forgot something. Ouch! Ouch! You didn't say "Thank you."

End of Scene

5

MONOLOGS
FOR MEN

A Lean, Mean, Singing Machine

Scene

A recital hall. Members of the Newton Community Chorus have gathered to practice for an upcoming event. Otto Gunther, gruff and ill mannered, barks commands as he enters from the wings. He makes his way to the edge of the stage to hold counsel with chorus members waiting in the auditorium.

OTTO GUNTHER: (*Entering—loudly*) Hey, you gotta move that box upstage. What? Hell no! I ain't no stage grip. Don't talk back to me. I said, don't talk back to me! We're gonna rehearse now ... so get the hell outta here. Now! Git! (*Gunther moves to the edge of the stage to address the chorus*)

All right, now. Listen up. All of you. Listen up! (*Finding a source of irritation*) Hey, when I say, "Listen up," I don't mean for you to keep yakking. So, just shut up and listen! (*Embracing all*) I'll ask the questions and you just nod your heads. I don't want to hear a single utterance from a single pie hole until we ... sing! You got that? (*Clearing the air*) All right. Now. Second question. All of you are card-carryin' members of the

Newton Community Chorus, am I right? (*Demonstrating*) Just nod. All right. Okay. Well, aren't you the lucky ones . . . because . . . let me introduce myself . . . I'm Otto Gunther . . . your new conductor. (*Matter-of-fact*) Randy ain't comin' back. Randy was fired. I don't know. They caught him with his pants down . . . down at the bus station. I don't know. But I'm the man now . . . and if'n you don't like it (*Showing his back*), here . . . you can pucker up and kiss my ham hocks as you walk out the door. (*He laughs*) Hahahaha!

So you decided to stay. Well, good for you. I'm not here to be your friend. I'm here to make a chorus! A lean, mean, singing machine. And we got only four weeks, four weeks, I said, to put the *Messiah* together. So hate me now . . . hate me later . . . but I'm gonna whip the *Messiah* out of you. (*Waving sheet music*) So, with no further adieu, let me introduce this oratorio supreme by the late, great, German composer George Frideric Handel, da man, and his *Messiah*, to the Newton Community Chorus.

Yep . . . but before I go on, there are a couple of things you need to know about me . . . Gunther. (*Choosing his words*) Firstly, you might hear some rumors . . . so let me set the record straight. It's true. I got in a fight once with a previous chorus member . . . in Scranton . . . a baritone. He thought he was a better conductor . . . thought he could run the show better than Gunther could. (*Making his case*) I was standin' in the wings . . . mindin' my own . . . peelin' an apple with a pocketknife . . . when the baritone accosted me. Well . . . to make a story short out of a long one, I accidentally sliced off a piece of his nose . . . and I regret that . . . but he's fine, and my insurance company paid for him to have a sporty little nose cap made of silver and gold. So, there's no hard feelings. It's in the past.

Now, secondly, I want you all to know my philosophy. So, question number three (*Raising his hand*): Do I have any strippers in the chorus? (*Slight pause*) I ask you, do any of you take off your clothes before an audience? (*Locating a pair of eyes*) Why are you lookin' at me like that? I don't mean G-strings and pasties . . . I mean the complete birthday suit . . . triple X, exposed . . . you know, like those monkeys on the Discovery Channel when they rise up and turn their butts to the camera and suddenly you're lookin' at this large, red, meaty . . . pustule. Now, that's exposed! That's naked! (*He laughs*) Hahahaha. And that's my philosophy. (*Emphatically*) Singin' before an audience is the same as strippin' before an audience. And so, my little songbirds, if you are ashamed of your . . . pustule . . . the Newton Community Chorus is not the place for you. (*He laughs*) Hahahaha. (*A sudden thought*) Hey, I didn't ask to walk upright . . . I was happy being a monkey . . . but since I'm standin' . . . we might as well sing.

All right. (*Waving the music—Gunther builds his vision for the piece with a high degree of emotion*) This is gonna take some fancy lip and lung action—it's a moody piece . . . one minute you're singin' all happy-like . . . voices are zippin' in and out of there . . . praisin' the glory of the Lord . . . and isn't this pure . . . and bring on the good stuff and ain't we havin' fun and then . . . bam! Shit hits the fan! And we're pissed off! And sad! And grievin'! And generally having a hell of a time comin' to grips with this whole Messiah mess . . . until . . . suddenly, suddenly, it all comes together and you can't help but be thrilled and so you sing out . . . you . . . the Newton Community Chorus . . . sing out! And you sing perfect! And in your vocal nakedness . . . you wash the audience with astonishment, as we all rise up and shout (*Singing*), "Hallelujah! Hallelujah! Hallelujah!" (*An abrupt stop*) Hey, hey, wait a minute! Bring down the curtain! Shit! I think I left my lights on . . . I'll be back in a minute. (*A quick exit*)

End of Scene

PETER PAN AND THE SQUARE-RIGGER

Scene

A stage. A technical rehearsal for a production of Peter Pan *is about to take place. Joel and his rigging crew are new arrivals to the production team. In fact, this may be the first time any of them have been in a theater. Joel and his crew are sailors, temporarily unemployed. Joel speaks with an Irish lilt as he steps toward the edge of the stage to talk to the production's technical director.*

JOEL: (*Searching the catwalks above the seating*) Captain Boker! They said you'd be walking the catwalks, fixing cable, and the like. I hope you don't mind me calling you Captain. It makes me feel at home, as if I were in deep water on a crack three-skysail-yarder. I want you to know, Captain, the stage is rigged and ready. (*Saluting*) Aye, aye, sir. When they told us down at the wharf that your theater here needed help with some rigging, the boys and I jumped at the opportunity to do a little good will. This community has been a good host to us . . . (*With a glimmer*) especially Sally Brown and her sisters. And since the *Henry B. Clipper* will not sail for a while, if ever again, God forbid, helping you out gives us a chance to be good neighbors.

    (*Assuming a sailor's posture—to his crew*) Coil up those ropes, a couple of you men! Heave ho! Give us a little shanty song while you work boys. Heave ho! (*To the technical director*) Aye, Captain. The boys and I always sing a little shanty while heaving up anchor or hoisting sails. And so I hope there are no rules about singing in the theater. (*A pleasant agreement*) I didn't think so. You know, Captain, when we showed up yesterday, the boys and I thought you wanted us to rope some block and tackles, rig some sails, or, I guess you call them, drapes. When I learned of your plans to fly real people around the stage, I thought, "Wallop me ass with a cannonball!

Theater people are crazy!" But then I watched the rehearsal of your play, *Peter Pan*, and I began to understand your determination. Just because we are no longer children, it doesn't mean we must give up on our dreams. It's an admirable thing you are doing, Captain. And so, just believe in my crew, and your Peter Pan and the Darlings will fly. (*Interrupted by his crew singing*) One moment, Captain. (*Commanding the crew*) Quiet, you scugs! Wallop me ass with a razor! That's a shitty tune you're singing. Now, sing the same song, boys! Newton! Your voice is running away from the others! Listen to them, Newton, and bring it together, or I'll be getting angry, lad. Now give it to us again, but this time all together.

(*To the technical director*) Sorry, Captain, but no two sailors ever sing the same shanty in quite the same way. Aye, but to do a job right, Captain, the boys have to sing and heave ho together. It is a performing art. Much like the theater, I daresay. I had never considered it before, but there is much we have in common: (*Looking around*) stage drapes like sails, ropes, rigging, running lights, and a crew and actors. Aye. (*With admiration*) A salty lot who have a difficult time keeping their feet on dry land . . . who, I imagine, are more at home in the exhilaration of a performance . . . a ship on the open sea. (*Heartfelt*) And so, Captain, if I could wish you one wish, it would be to stand on the polished teak forecastle of a ship in deep water. A square-rigger with her sails full, like healthy young lungs, from jib to spanker, sails, fore and aft, riding a nor'eastern trade wind, making time, bound to some exotic port. Aye. (*Truthfully*) It is an artful life to be a sailor on a real ship. But I'm sorry to say, there isn't much of a demand . . . for square-rigged . . . sailors. I wish the theater better success, Captain. (*Again interrupted by the crew singing*)

Quiet! Newton! The tune! The tune! Don't make me ashamed of our performance. If your singing isn't in tune with the others, you will drop that little Peter Pan on her arse. (*Taking control of the situation*) Boys, it seems the "Highland

Laddie" is too difficult for Newton. Let's try "Blow the Man Down." Heave away, you men—let's hear some noise! (*Singing*)

Come all you young fellows who follow the sea,
To me way, hay, blow the man down, (*Shouting*, "Pull!")
Now, please pay attention and listen to me,
Give me some time to blow the man down! ("Pull!")

End of Scene

A Seamless Pitch

Scene

The beach. Allen and Angela, high-school students, are skipping pebbles along the top of the water. Angela is an exchange student from Africa with very little knowledge of English. Undeterred by the language barrier, Allen instructs Angela in the art of skipping stones.

ALLEN: (*Watching Angela's throw*) Ooh! One, two, three. Three skips, Angela. That's good, but you've got to find the right pebble . . . flat and smooth. (*Locating a pebble*) That throw looked like a knuckleball, the way it took off to the right. I bet one side of that pebble was scuffed up, so when you threw it, the wind caught the rough side, forcing it out of balance. (*Handing her a pebble*) Try again. Ready? One, two, ka-plunk!! No, no, Angela, did you see the way it sank just before it hit the water? (*Showing the hand position*) You threw a split-finger toss. You need the perfect pebble, a seamless pitch, and the right wind conditions for a split finger. But keep it up, Angela, you've got a good arm.

Do they play baseball in Africa? I'm sorry. I'm so stupid. I hope you don't mind me just talking. I know it's awkward. I know you don't understand what I'm saying. So, just put hands over your ears . . . like this (*Covering his ears*) . . . if you want me to shut up. (*Spotting his dog, Newton*) Hey, look at Newton. He's chasing a seagull. He almost caught it! (*Calling out*) Newton, leave the bird alone! (*To Angela*) Newton doesn't get out too often. We have to keep him in our fenced-in backyard, so he's pretty excited to run on the beach. He loves it here. So do I. (*Sitting on the beach*)

The ocean is amazing. And today it's so calm. (*With some excitement*) Wouldn't it be great, Angela, if you could skip a pebble all the way from the shores of America to the shores of Africa . . . to your hometown . . . what is it . . . now, don't tell me . . . I know it. Port Gentil in Gabon. It sounds like an incredible place. And hot! I can't believe you live on the equator . . . zero degrees latitude . . . the equator! It must be scorching! I'm out in the sun five minutes and I look like boiled shrimp! (*Studying her*) But your skin is perfect, and your eyes . . . (*Disrupted*) Newton! (*Standing to call out*) Leave that bird alone! He's such a dumb dog when he gets out like this. Stupid dog! Ha! (*An innocent confession*) I should talk, Angela. Look at me. I don't know very much about the world or anything. I didn't even know that your native language is French until just the other day . . . not that that it matters . . . not that I could speak it. (*Slight laugh*) What I do know is baseball and, well . . . I like to read . . . novels and poetry.

Believe it or not, I really enjoy our English lit class . . . *Hamlet* and all that . . . but it's kind of strange because you have to pretend like you don't like it . . . because . . . well . . . well . . . it's Shakespeare . . . and so . . . I don't know. I don't know why I have to pretend, Angela. It's stupid, isn't it? (*With newfound awareness*) If you like something . . . or someone . . . why should you pretend that you don't? (*Recalling the past*) I still remember the first day you walked into our class. We were reading a scene from *Romeo and Juliet* . . . the party scene . . . everyone was wearing these construction-paper masks . . . we had made a few minutes earlier. Romeo was describing Juliet to Tybalt . . . and suddenly you appeared in the doorway (*Enjoying the memory*) . . . I don't know . . . like a vision . . . like it was planned or something. And then Romeo said: (*Reciting the speech with sincerity*)

O, She doth teach the torches to burn bright!
It seems she hangs upon the cheek of night
As a rich jewel in an Ethiop's ear—
Beauty too rich for use, for earth too dear.

You took an empty seat next to me. (*A wash of emotion*) I . . . ahh . . . was afraid to look at you . . . to catch your eye . . . but when I did . . . you smiled. I thought . . . *she likes me . . . hey . . . I think she likes me.* And then . . . I remembered . . . I was wearing this mask . . . it was kind of a rabbit's face . . . pink ears . . . and buck teeth . . . and it hit me that it might not be me you like . . . but the rabbit. So . . . I was stuck for the rest of that class, afraid to take off the mask, wondering what you would think if you saw the real me. (*Slight laugh*) That's pretty stupid, isn't it? (*Watching her throw a pebble*)

Five skips. Great, Angela. Now, throw this one with more sidearm, a little backspin, and a snap of the wrist. (*Demonstrating*) Like this. Some day, Angela, I'm going to visit your country . . . and we will stand on the beach at Port Gentil and skip stones toward America. (*Sudden alarm*) Oh no, Newton! He caught the bird! (*Chasing off after Newton*) Newton! Drop that seagull, now!

End of Scene

THE 1ST DEAD MAN IN GROVER'S CORNERS

Scene

A dress rehearsal for a production of Thornton Wilder's Our Town. *The actors are reaching the end of the play. Emily has just returned to her grave from a day with the living to resume her place in the cemetery. True to Wilder's minimal use of properties, the graveyard is represented by actors/characters sitting on chairs. The scene picks up with the 1st Dead Man's line, which is also the cue for George to make his final entrance.*

1ST DEAD MAN: (*Reciting lines from the play*) "And my Joel, who knew the stars—he used to say it took millions of years for that little speck o' light to git down to earth. Don't seem like a body could believe it, but that's what he used to say—millions of years." (*Awkward pause—the actor playing the 1st Dead Man begins to ad-lib*)

Aya, millions of years. (*Pause*) Yes sir. My boy Joel was a sailor. I wanted him to be a doctor, like your husband, Mrs. Gibbs. But no, Joel wouldn't think of that. He loved water. Boats. And the big sky. Aya, knew all the stars. All those little specks o' light. (*Pause*) Millions. Constellations. (*Pause. Again, he begins to ad-lib*) Ursa Major. Ursa Minor. Cassiopeia. Andromeda. Well now, Emily has just revisited her earthly home and bid her final fare-thee-well to the world. Aya, that just about does it for me as well. Clocks ticking. Her butternut tree. Coffee. Hot baths! (*Beginning to break character*) Did I say clocks ticking . . . hot chocolate . . . and stupid actors! (*Contemptuously, the actor breaks out of character and begins to scold the director*)

Where's George? How long, Ludwig? How long do I sit here ad-libbing with egg on my face? Do you really think I can improve on Mr. Wilder's play? (*Stands and yells*) Hey, Stage Manager, go find the real stage manager and tell him to find

Newton! (*Steps toward the edge of the stage to chastise the director further*) You know, Ludwig, we open in three nights, and we have not had one complete run-through. I don't want to say I told you so, but didn't I tell you so? It was a mistake casting Newton as George. He's a nitwit, Ludwig! (*His resentment grows*) He's always late for rehearsal, and when he is here, he can't deliver the same line in the same place twice. And when he goes up, he stands there with this stupid grin on his face, making it seem like the rest of us don't know our lines. Aya, I'm fed up with the dumb-cluck. I don't care what you think, Ludwig, and forgive me, because I know you studied at a studio in New York, and I respect that, but that Newton is no actor. It's shameful what he is doing to this beautiful play and the rest of us.

(*Pointedly*) Admit it, Ludwig. There's no emotion in anything he says. Take this scene, for example: When he shows up here in the graveyard, you directed him, Ludwig, to drop to his knees beside Emily's grave. Right? The fresh grave, for crying out loud, of his prematurely departed young wife, and you told him to weep, convulsively. Guess what, Ludwig? He's laughing! You can't see his face because he's looking upstage most of the time . . . but everyone in the graveyard can see him. (*Turning to the others in the graveyard scene*) Right, Mrs. Gibbs, Simon Stimsom, right? Second Dead Man? Am I right? (*Turning back to the director*) He's laughing! (*Incredulously*) His wife, poor Emily, has just died giving birth to his child, and he thinks it's a laugh riot! (*Letting it all out*) The guy has a bad attitude and he's ruining *Our Town*. Ruining it! It's shameful. He has no respect for this play or for any of us here. Let me tell you something else, Ludwig: This is going to be the worst production of *Our Town* in the history of community theater. Hey, I know I'm just the First Dead Man, but I've put a lot of hours into this production, and I think I am speaking for all the dead . . . here. Right, folks? (*Decisively*) I can't act with him anymore! And another thing, the stage manager is a deadhead . . . not the actor . . . the real one . . . and I think he's smoking something weird. (*Spotting a child in the wings*)

Hey! Hey! Tycho! (*Ordering*) Don't touch the counter-weight system! Stay away from that electric winch. You're going to drop a full batten of lighting instruments and kill everyone in the graveyard. Tycho! Get away from there! (*He turns on the actor playing Emily, who also happens to be Tycho's mother*) You know, Emily, that kid of yours doesn't need to be running around backstage, making a nuisance of himself. And don't give me that crap about (*Quoting the play*) "People don't understand. And how troubled and dark our lives are." That kid is a nuisance . . . a regular Dennis the Menace . . . and if I catch him in my dressing room again, I'm going to slice off a piece of his nose. What kind of a name is "Tycho," anyway? What is his father? A Lego toy? Where are you from, anyway?

(*To the director*) Hey, Ludwig, don't you have a rule about outsiders at rehearsal? (*The director is leaving the theater*) Hey, where are you going? Ludwig, are we taking a break? Because, if this is a break, I didn't have a chance to eat before I came. I need some nourishment. I'm not staying in this graveyard any longer . . . this place stinks! (*He turns on everyone and speaks with a New England dialect*) Aya, you all stink! I'm going down to the green room, and, guess what? I'm making a huge pot of New England clam chowder. Aya. Enough for all. (*Mockingly*) Then we call all sit around the green room table, chat, and sip soup, because in *Our Town*, we like to know the real facts about everybody in Grover's Corners. For example, is Tycho really a boy, or a devil child? Actors . . . my . . . my, isn't theater awful—and wonderful? I'll be in the green room if you want me.

End of Scene

DODGEBALL MATADOR

Scene

An open gym room. A required high-school P.E. class is in session. Adam and other students are in the middle of a dodgeball game, clearly one of Adam's least favorite activities. He finds some assurance in sharing his frustration with Newton, a friend, while also pretending that the game is a bullfight and that he is a matador.

ADAM: *Ahhhhhhhh, toro, mira, toro, ahhhhh.* Whoa! That was close. *Viva la . . . matador!* (*To Newton*) I hate this game, Newton. I'm going to get donked any minute now. And it isn't fair! If I'm donked again, I have to go to the third-tier team, and that means I'll be lucky to get a C in this crappy course! Watch it, Newton! (*A ball is hurled*) Watch it! (*Dodging*) *Olé*! Before class I asked Tandy if he was giving us one of his little *quizzees* today, and without changing expression, he said, "No, Adam, I'm giving you one of my big *testes!*"

Watch out, Newton, Joe is taking aim. (*Dodging the ball*) *Olé!* Good move, Newton. You know, I haven't slept in weeks, and my grades are slipping, and I can't breathe! I feel like Piggy in *Lord of the Flies!* After all these years of school, Newton, higher math, language studies, and years of Spanish, my diploma now depends on my ability to dodge a ball. It isn't fair! This is a nightmare, a war zone. That's right, Newton, it's war! And I'll not stand here like some pathetic pacifist while the commander and his squadrons of Ritalin addicts add me to their death count. I'm fighting back, Newton!

(*Calling out*) *Ahhhhhhhh, toro, mira, toro, ahhhhh.* Throw the ball, cheesehead! I've read Hemingway's *Death in the Afternoon,* and if I must fight . . . (*Striking a pose*) I will fight with dignity . . . without fear. And if you gouge me, I will not show surprise . . . or anguish. No more jerky little movements because . . . I am elegance and beauty. The essence of rhythm and grace, the matador! (*Dodging the ball*) *Olé*! Aha! Your little ball missed me. Weenies! Before you engage in the *corrida de toros*, a complete bullfight with a real matador, perhaps you and your little boys should practice with the *novillada*, the amateurs in middle school. *Ahhhhhhhh, toro, mira, toro, ahhhh.* (*Dodging again*) Aha! You missed again! Aha! And now I will defeat you with a very basic pass, the *veronica*. (*He is the matador*) Holding my cape so gently by the corners, as if wiping the face of Jesus on the Cross, I will cite, pass, and complete this move. *Ahhhhhhhh, toro, mira, toro, ahhhh. Olé!* Ha, ha, ha, ha! And now the *hora de la verdad*, the hour of truth. And when I am done, Newton, I will cut off the bull's testicles, I will roast them on an open fire, and I will eat them. Yummy!

Watch it, Newton! (*Newton is hit*) Ouch! *Que tal, amigo?* That must have hurt. Ahhh, my *banderillero*—and now that you are out, I tip my hat and say, *Va por ti.* This one is for you. The kill. *Ahhhhhhhh, toro, mira, toro.* Lifting my *muleta* and concealing the *matar*, I will not stand, *recibiendo*, and wait for the bull to charge. No, my friend, I will charge the waiting bull, *volapie*, and with flying feet, I will run like hell to the locker room. Wait! What do you know? Ha, ha, ha. There is fear in the bull's eyes, Newton. See it? Yes . . . fear. He knows now . . . that he is . . . defeated. *Olé*!

(*Dropping the affectation*) Oh, no . . . what's he doing! Ohh, no, ohh . . . yuck . . . he's throwing . . . up . . . booting . . . all over Tandy's shoes. Ahh! What a mess! This is gross! Disgusting! Who's going to clean that up? (*Announcing loudly*) You know, Mr. Tandy, they really shouldn't schedule P.E. after lunch. Hey, there's the bell. *Viva el matador*! I guess this means, I win. *Olé* ! Hey, Newton, did you study for that health quiz?

End of Scene

BOTTOM'S DREAM

Scene

The bleachers. It is the bottom of the last inning at a regional high-school baseball game. George Bottom, a serious, overly expressive fan, sits in the bleachers with his quiet friend, Newt. George's team is in the field and his young idol, Jake, is on the mound.

GEORGE BOTTOM: (*To Newt*) Ha! Yeah! See it break? Sweet and smooth. Just like I told you he could do! The kid's a dream, Newt. A dream. (*Encouraging the pitcher, Jake, loudly*) Now, come on, Jake, come on, you gotta fight back now, and get 'em. Just one time. Hard! Rock and fire! Pop! Oh, mother of God! Whew! And that's three! Yeah, daddy! (*The batter throws down his bat in anger*) Hey! Hey! Hey! He can't do that! (*Yelling at the umpire*) Hey, fat boy, tell him! He can't do that! That's unsportsmanlike. It's unsportsmanlike behavior, throwing a bat. He can't do that, fat boy! Toss his skinny butt out of the park! (*Surprised by the umpire's remark*) What? Don't tell me to take it easy. Do your job, fat boy, and take control of this situation! Someone's gonna get hurt, you hear me?! And it just might be you!

(*Turning back to Newt*) He's a dream, Newt. A dream. Nothing shakes him. He's sweet and smooth. (*To the pitcher*) This one likes to bunt, Jake! Don't give it to him! Rock and fire! Pop! (*A strike*) That a boy! Make him stand tall and take the heat like the rest of 'em. Come on, now. Two more. Mix it up! (*Another strike*) Oh, yeah! Slap! That was pretty, boy. Snappy, sweet, and smooth. Right, Newt? Newt! It's the last inning, the bottom of the last inning. One out, just two more, and it's all over. So take your nose outta that book, Newt, and watch your friend throw.

Here we go. Here we go, here we go, here . . . we . . . Pop! (*Strike three*) He's outta here! Sweet! Two down . . . and one to go! Make it . . . one to go! Make it . . . one to go! Hey, fat boy . . . make it . . . one to go! Make it . . . one to go! (*Back to Newt*) Newt? Are you with me? Jake is about to make the most important out in all of Central High School baseball, and what are you doing? Drawing pictures. Look, boy, look and learn. (*To the pitcher*) Watch it now, watch it. He likes the inside and he's a sucker for a high one. Just give 'em your stuff. Rock and fire! And . . . it's . . . (*Strike one*) one! Slap leather! Pretty pitch! The kid's a dream. Two more and let's go home!

Let me see that picture, Newt. Give it here. (*George grabs Newt's drawing pad. To the pitcher*) Pull back, stretch, and throw hard. Give him a big target, Catch. (*Strike two*) Yeah. Pop. Slap leather. And . . . it's . . . two! A dream. All right, Newt, what is this? What are you drawing? (*Surprised by the drawing*) Hey, that's me, you drew a picture of me . . . my head . . . on . . . what looks like . . . a jackass. What is this! (*Reading the caption under the caricature*) "Methought I was enamour'd of an ass." Shakespeare. (*Staring at Newt*) For crying out loud, Newt. What are you trying to do? Shake my confidence? Here it is, the last pitch in regional action, and you call me a jackass! (*Showing some anger*) Damn! Well . . . damn! Well . . . it'll take more than a little picture to shake the ol' nerves of George Bottom.

(*To the pitcher*) Now, here we go, here we go. Rock and fire! Yeah! Nice pitch! What?! (*Incredulously*) A ball? Did he say a ball?! (*Yelling at the umpire*) You are a horse's ass, fat boy. A fat jackass that needs glasses! You wouldn't know a strike if it hit you between the jackass eyes, fat boy! (*Rising in indignation*) What? You can't throw me out! You can't do that! You can't stop the game like this. The game is bigger than you, fat boy. Put on that mask, squat down a few inches, if you can, and call the strike. (*Slight pause*) Well . . . you gonna do it? (*He sits*) No . . . well . . . we'll just sit here then. We'll just sit right here. We'll just see. We'll just see.

End of Scene

FIE UPON'T!

Scene

A theater. A production of Hamlet *is about to take place, and Henri, the stage manager (and a frustrated actor), is calling places. Newton, Henri's assistant stage manager, has been told he will perform tonight as an understudy. Henry stops to offer some advice to the player.*

HENRI: "Speak the speech, I pray you." (*To Newton*) It's all about courage and talent . . . and . . . well, you have a lot of courage . . . Newton. Just remember to hold your head up and . . . well . . . project. Acting Shakespeare requires just a little . . . dignity . . . and a lot of emotion. And I don't know what you heard in the green room, damn it, but I'm not angry with you, friend. *Carpe diem.*

Oh, by the way, five minutes. (*Lacking total sincerity*) But . . . don't lose your nerve now, Newton. And don't think about the audience . . . it's only . . . well . . . two hundred and fifty people, maybe more. But just listen to me. (*Instructing*) Take a deep breath and say, "Inhale my body." Good. (*Performing the breathing exercise with Newton*) And now let it out slowly: "Exhale my body." Again, "Inhale my body" and "Exhale my body." It's all about courage and emotion and talent. And whether you know it or not, you have some of those things. (*Breathing in*) "Inhale."

The actors like you, Newton. I see it in the way they respond when you yell "Places!" with such affection. Exhale . . . damn it . . . you can do this. You've been my assistant . . . assistant stage manager since the beginning. (*With growing frustration*) You know every word, every movement, every pause, and every . . . thing . . . because . . . I taught you. (*Uncontrollably*) I taught you . . . everything, and now . . . you will walk out there . . . to applause . . . and once again, I . . . will . . . not. And . . . I admit . . . it hurts. (*Exclaiming*) *Stop the World, I Want to Get Off*! Oh, oh, Newton, if he had only seen me in that show . . . he would know . . . yes . . . he would know. (*Venting his emotions*) "Fie upon't! Foh!"

I'm just a little upset, Newton, that the director asked you and not me to take over this role. What experience have you had? (*Reaching Hamlet's emotional conclusion*) "What would he do had he the motive and the cue for passion that I have?" (*Turning on Newton*) I mean, you're a first-year student, Newton, and I've been a member of the Studio for almost three . . . if you count summer stock . . . which I do. I've paid my dues and even adopted a stage name, Henri with an "i". It's just not fair. Inhale. (*He does*) "Fie upon't!" (*Letting loose*) I know he doesn't like me. He has his pet actors. I think he's sleeping with Ophelia . . . oh, it makes me mad. And if I complain, I'll never be cast. You see, I can say nothing, Newton. Except, "Bloody, bawdy villain! Remorseless, treacherous, lecherous, kindless villain!"

There. Exhale. (*Regaining control*) Whew! I feel better now. I'm sorry you had to hear that, Newton . . . but if you act around here . . . I mean, if you are going to be an actor in this theater . . . you must learn to perform . . . fearlessly . . . boldly . . . and without a net. And remember what the flying Karl Wallenda said: "The dead are gone, and the show must go on." So, places, Newton . . . and . . . break a leg.

End of Scene

Rein in the Sterling Sphinxes

Scene

A small-town parade. Mitchell Gray and his friend, Newton, have entered a float in the parade in hopes of winning the competition. Mitchell and Newton stop their float at the judges' station, and Mitchell steps out to deliver his prepared speech for the judges.

Mitchell Gray: (*In confidence*) Newton, stop the float! We're at the judges' grandstand. Now, stop the float, Newton! Put it in park and don't move until you hear me say, "Give us light." (*Stepping forward and reciting his speech with mechanical precision*)

We celebrate this day, during the annual Popcorn Day Festival, honoring a tradition that started thousands of years ago: the parade of the ancient procession of the god Up-wa-wet. Like all who have paraded, yesterday and today, we move in a straight line, very slowly, so as not to bump into each other. My friend and I have put on a great show to celebrate the parade's theme: "The Past Meets the Future: Say Hooray for Popcorn Day!" (*Ceremoniously*) Up-wa-wet, we praise thee, and, we thank the city fathers and these smart judges for this opportunity to display our float, designed by Newton and Gray. Hooray for Popcorn Day!

(*Guiding the judges*) Please note: Our float is truly a float. It isn't pulled by animals, like those that have gone before us, or by tractors, like those that will follow. Ours ... really ... floats. (*Instructing*) Note how it glides, effortlessly, graciously, onward, as these two sculptured, shiny Egyptian sphinxes, harnessed to this silver NASA rocket, all surrounded by a metallic heat shield, and all made completely of recycled aluminum foil and chicken wire, connect the myths of our past to the mysteries of our future. Hooray for Popcorn Day! (*With humility*) And thank you. Judges, we hope you are pleased with our entry. (*Moving to his seat*)

Now it is time to blast off, and so I will take my seat in the silver-gilded cockpit and rein in the sterling sphinxes, and ask the god Up-wa-wet to show you his power. Light the way from the tip of the great lion-man's head to the tail of this spacecraft. Bring us light! (*He pauses*) And give us speed so that we may escape the pull of gravity from this solid earth. Bring us light, Up-wa-wet! Once more, bring us light! (*Whispering*) Newton, turn on the generator. Up-wa-wet, send us your sign. Bring us light! (*Again, whispering*) Newton, turn on the switch. Start the lights and popcorn balloons.

(*To the judges*) It is not every day that the past and the present float into the future. So, Up-wa-wet, bring us . . . Shit! (*He jumps*) Ouch! Ouch! (*Being shocked*) Shit! Newton, turn it off. Shit! Damn! (*Wild and terrified*) You're shocking me, Newton. Ouch! Damn! Shit! There's a short! The foil! Ouch! Shocking! Ouch! Jesus! Newton, turn off the damn generator! The whole damn float is electric! (*Yelling*) Turn it off! The switch! The switch! Turn off the switch! I'm frying up here! Christ! I'm frying! (*Pause. The shock is over*) There. Okay. Thank God. It . . . has . . . stopped. It is over. Okay. That's it. Okay, Newton. Don't move. I'm getting down. So . . . don't . . . I'm telling you . . . don't touch a thing until both of my feet are on solid earth. (*Walking away from the seat*) There. (*Signing relief. Suddenly aware of the judges*) Ummm . . . well . . . that's it. Okay, Newton, move it. (*Exiting*) Here comes a tractor.

End of Scene

THE LINE-UP

Scene

A stage. An audition. Barry Gascon, a guy in his early twenties, walks conspicuously onto the stage. This place, the theater, and the people seated in the audience begin a new experience for Barry, and he proceeds initially with a high degree of suspicion.

BARRY GASCON: (*Clearing his throat, Barry talks directly to the casting directors in the audience*) Okay, now, ahh . . . the rosy spandex girl . . . there . . . in the wings . . . with the clipboard . . . and the nice muffins . . . said . . . I'm . . . ahh . . . supposed to say my name first and then this . . . here number. (*Referring to a number pinned to his shirt*) Is that right? (*Nodding*) Well . . . the name is . . . Barry Gascon. And I'm . . . ahh . . . (*Checking his number*) numero twenty-five. So there.

(*All business*) Let's get something straight here. I don't belong to the lavender club. I mean, if I'm gonna engage in a little tongue sushi today . . . it's going to be with the rosy spandex girl and not with none of you yodelers. I don't yodel . . . and . . . I don't dance . . . well . . . that ain't exactly true. I do dance a little . . . you know, "Rompin' Molly" or that . . . ahh . . . "Pigtown Hoe Down," but I need a lot of room for that, so that's another story.

To be honest with you, I've never done nothin' like this before . . . and so if you don't want me . . . just do a little preemptive strike here . . . it won't break my heart. I belong to the Union. I have friends. I'm walkin' tall. It ain't like I'm just dyin' to be here . . . you know. I ain't that . . . ahh . . . actor Richard Dreyfus in the movie, ahhhh, *Close Encounters of the Third Kind*, where he gets all crazy, you know, rippin' up bushes and tossin' buckets of sand and mud in his livin' room, tellin' his lovely wife to kiss off, all because he's got this . . . obsession . . . with that . . . ahh . . . mountain . . . you know, some Devil-somethin' Mountain out in godforsaken, dirt Nevada. No . . . it ain't an obsession . . . with me.

I'm here today because . . . well . . . (*Not too happy about this*) Newton, my parole officer, said, "Barry, you goin' to do some community service when you get out." Well, I ain't pickin' up garbage or watchin' some old fart drool at the old geezers' home . . . but when I saw your announcement . . . about community theater . . . I asked Newton, "Newton, do you think . . . community theater is community service?" (*Shrugging*) And since he didn't have a good answer . . . I'm here. But . . . ahh . . . Newton did say I would have to read somethin' . . . or recite somethin' . . . and I noticed the actor before me, number twenty-four, was like . . . acting his cojones off. (*Offering surprise*) I mean, I really thought he was gonna beat up on that girl he was acting with . . . here. And when he started yellin' (*Imitating the actor*) "Stella! Stella!" It looked like he was gonna upchuck right here on the floor! (*Total disbelief*) Right here! Mother Mary! (*Startled*) Look! Look-a here! There is a puddle of sweat right here on the stage floor! The guy must have been sweatin' like a horse . . . I mean, you saw him, right? (*Heavily involved*) He looked like an animal. And the way he growled (*Growling*), "Stella!" "Stell-lahhhhh!" It sent chills right down my spine . . . and into my flat feet. Listen to me, I know. I've seen fireworks in my time . . . but nothin' . . . nothin' . . . was more thrillin' than that moment. (*Emphatically*) That man is an actor! You should use him. Listen to me! But now it's gone! He's gone! All that emotion . . . is just a memory! And what did he leave behind? This puddle of sweat! This puddle! (*Slight pause*)

Wait a minute! You don't think the girl peed herself, do you? Naaah, it's sweat. The man is an actor! You know, you gotta use him in this production. (*Taking over*) You got his phone number? His line-up number was . . . ahh . . . twenty-four . . . and I think his name was Marvin or Stanley. Listen, I'll do you a favor.

I'll call him back out here. (*Shouting*) Hey, Chum! Marvin! Stanley! (*Looking in the wings*) Guess he's gone. Too bad.

Hey, you know, I kinda' like this theater thing. Standing up here . . . on the stage . . . shoutin' . . . at the top of my voice. It kinda frees you up, you know, what they call . . . therapeutic. Makes you feel good. Tell you what. Go ahead. Sign me up. I'll do your play. And now, as a bonus, I'm gonna do a little "Rompin' Molly"—or maybe you'd rather see my "Pigtown Hoe Down." They're both good. (*He dances*)

End of Scene

SHORTY'S OLD MAN'S BOARD
OR S'UP?

Scene

Downtown parking lot. Slick, a teenage boy, glides onto the scene on his skateboard with great dexterity and skill. Flipping and grinding, he approaches his skateboarding friend, Newt, bringing his board to a halt. Newt, silent, is clearly preoccupied with repairing the wheels on his skateboard.

SLICK: S'up, Newt, a.k.a. Hawk? Who're you schooling today? (*Noticing Newt's board*) Whoa! Where did ya' get them wheels, dude? They're like ancient or somethin'. Yeah, that must have been Shorty's old man's board or somethin'. No grip, no trucks, just a plywood deck and roll-about wheels, man. It's a classic, old school. Rock and roll. (*Playfully*) You should take it to the Antiques Roadshow and check its value. Like, you could hand it to some old dude in a bow tie. He'll do a couple of flip tricks on it and say, "Where did you get this board?" (*Enjoying the game*) And you'll say, "It belonged to Shorty's old man." He'll raise his eyebrows and say, "Do you have any idea what this is worth?" And you'll say, "It has a lot of sentimental value." He'll smile, lift his nose, and announce: "It's worth $27,342. Congratulations." And you're, like, stoked man, and you'll sell it to him right there because you know it's junk, and then go out and buy some real wheels. (*Catching his breath*)

Whoa, Newt, did you see the news? City passed a law against boarders. Said the cops can ticket us, man, if they catch us on public property, like right here and now, downtown. I say, let 'em try to catch us. (*Playfully*) We'd smoke 'em, flip, slide, and glide away. (*Again checking out Newt's board*) But not on that thing. Not on Shorty's old man's board. The thing is ass-out dangerous, with those metal skates, you know what I mean? You hit just a little rock, dude, like a pebble, and the skate will nose-grind and flip your ass back to the future. I am not kidding, Newt. I wouldn't do it. (*Shaking his head*) Well, yeah, I know you're like, (*Imitating Newt*) "Nothing can happen to me, man, I know every crack in the concrete, every bump in the road. Like it's my cosmic highway I ride all day, every day, dude, eternal and never changing." It's like Newt's laws of skateboarding motion. (*Startled by Newt's movement toward the top of the hill*)

Wait! No way, man! Not down Nollie's Hill, dude. Not now, man, it's rush hour, and not unless you have a high tolerance for pain. Not unless you're Superman or somethin', 'cause you gonna die, dude, if you do that! You hear me? You gonna die! And I'll have to go knock on your door (*Rapping on his board*), and your old lady, wringing her hands on a wash towel, will answer: "He ain't here, Slick." And I'll have to say, "You're telling me! The last time I saw him, he tried an indy grab down Nollie's Hill, and now he's, like, roadkill or something, with ten toes up!" She gets all whacked and emotional and starts dissing on me about boarders, and I don't need to hear that from your old lady, Newt. (*Trying to assert himself*) So give me the board, Newt. Give it here. (*Demanding*) You can't ride it down Nollie, and that's it! Not on that piece of junk! Not now. Not while Slick's here. (*Startled by Newt's movement down the hill*)

Newt! Newt! Don't do it! Dude, you're crazy! Watch the car, man! And that old . . . dog . . . Whoa! (*Impressed*) Nice curb slide. Phat and smooth. (*Becoming involved in play-by-play action*) No! No! Yes! A . . . rail slide . . . and . . . launch! Wow! He's airborne! Shovit, Newt! Shovit, again! Look at him go! Look at that! Amazing! (*With great fanfare*) He's going aerial. He's aiming for the tailgate of the pickup truck . . . and he lands a perfect handplant invert, which was fresh, man, out of the pack! Incredible! (*Celebratory*) Come on, now, give in up for Newt! Give it up! Give it up! Give it up! (*Sudden surprise*) Whoa, oh, no, Newt, there's a cop on a horse. Where did he come from? (*Calling out*) Newt, turn around! There's a cop on a horse! Turn around! Watch the horse! Flip it around, Newt! (*Wincing*) Ohhhh . . . right up the horse's . . . ouchhh . . . giddy-up . . . ummm . . . (*To himself*) that must've hurt. (*To Newt*) Great ride, dude! (*Slick flips his board and glides away*)

End of Scene

STYLING WITH WILLIAM

Scene

A cafeteria in a student union building. Rosen, a student, has just returned from an unsuccessful meeting with his literature professor. He tosses his backpack on the floor and takes a seat across from a friend and fellow student, Newton.

ROSEN: "It's all in your head," he said. I'm flunking the class, Newton, and he tells me, "It's all in my head!" He won't give me an extension. He said it wasn't fair to the rest of you clowns in the class. Then he goes off on this lecture about memory blocks, and Ronald Reagan, drugs, alcohol, mind over matter, Aristotle's heart, and the human computer, and something . . . weird . . . about the Grateful Dead, whatever! He shoots more words and I nod and nod and finally he says, "Do you understand, Mr. Rosen?" and I say, "Yes, I do." But I don't. (*Unzipping his backpack and retrieving a Shakespeare text*) I know he knows that I don't and so I say, "No, I don't really understand." And he says, "Why did you say you did, Mr. Rosen?" And I say, "I don't know." "Oh," he says, with his chin in his hand and an expression on his face like: "This boy is stupid." Then I blurt out, "But I'm not stupid!" (*Opening the book*) "I'm having a hard time memorizing this speech, that's all! I need an extension!" "No extensions," he snaps. "If Napoleon could greet thousands of his soldiers by name, you should be able to recite one of Shakespeare's little speeches."

The man's a tyrant, Newton, and I fart at him and his old English! And I'm sick of his class. (*Slamming the book shut*) And I'm sick of this school! I'm sick of it! Hell, I'd rather skateboard to the nearest McJob and spend my off time rewinding *Oprah.*

Do you know what he calls us? (*Not allowing Newton time to respond*) "Loose chippings." That's right. Yeah, well, I looked it up the other day, Newton, and you know what "loose chippings" means in the Old Queen's English? "Rocks" or "gravel" or something like that! And that's what he thinks of us . . . of me . . . I'm just some loose gravel or dirt he walks on . . . and intimidates. (*Rising*) I'm sick of his insults . . . his academic terrorism . . . making me feel . . . like dog shit, like a biohazard, like something . . . unworthy. That's it! (*Fully and expressively—Hamlet*) Like the man said, "How unworthy a thing you make of me! You would play upon me, you would seem to know my stops, you would pluck out the heart of my mystery, you would sound me from my lowest note to the top of my compass—and there is much music, excellent voice, in this little organ—yet cannot you make it speak. 'Sblood, do you think I am easier to be played on than a pipe? Call me what instrument you will; though you can fret me, you cannot play upon me." (*Amazed—sitting*)

Gawd! I did it! Newton, that's it. I know the speech. I know it! I don't need an extension, Newton, I'm busting on the scene and I need an audience. I just blurted it out! You heard it. Out! Out . . . of . . . my brain and my heart, and for a moment I felt down with Hamlet, in tune with the man . . . styling! Styling with William! Let the class begin! (*Rosen collects his book and backpack and begins to leave*) Newton, say, do you need help with your speech?

End of Scene

Hamlet, Act III, sc. ii, lines 380–390.

HALLEY'S FAT STRAT

Scene

A rock 'n' roll concert stage. Eddie, a young man, college age, is laying cable, connecting microphones, and testing the sound levels before the evening's concert. Eddie is an aspiring guitarist, and he can easily see himself as a lead guitarist taking center stage as a rock 'n' roll star.

EDDIE HALLEY: (*Speaking into a microphone*) Check. Check. This is Eddie Halley . . . testing, sliding on a moonbeam. Testing. One, two. Check. (*Looking out into the audience for Newt, a lighting technician, working a follow spot on a tower*) Hey, Newt! We're tweaking the levels on these three mics, and then you can run your lights. Testing, one, two, check. Mic number one, check. "Chuck Berry is here to stay"—testing. "And when he plays that Johnny song,"—testing, "my air guitar begins to sway." (*Playing air guitar to "Johnny B. Good"*) So, "Go, go, Johnny, go, go, go, de, de, de, de, de. Go, Johnny, go, go, go . . . " (*He stops suddenly and moves to the next microphone*) Aaahrightie, that's smooth, let's lay down a groove on mic number two.

Hey, Newt, did I tell you? The band offered me a tour with 'em . . . as a roadie. It's cool! I dig this band and I like their music . . . it's more booty-shaking then head-banging . . . which is good, 'cause I'm growin' out of the metalhead period in my life. Besides they've got one bad-ass guitarist . . . Louie. You just wait till you hear him tonight, Newt. I swear, he shreds the ass off of that beautiful '57 Fiesta Red Fat Strat he wears. And what passion! Man, where can you learn that? (*Working it out*) But it means I . . . ah . . . won't be goin' back to school next fall, but . . . ah . . . that's okay, because, well, the dean and I didn't seem to agree on the meanin' of my GPA.

It's crazy, Newt. You know Seaberry, my roommate? Plugged in and burned out, he never picked up a book, partied like an animal, skipped classes, drove to Mexico the week before exams . . . and man, at the end of the semester . . . he made the dean's list . . . while I'm on . . . well . . . the dean's shit list! And now (*He sings*) "My daddy don't dance, and my mama don't rock 'n' roll." (*Emphatically*) And the thing is, Newt, I studied! I mean, I really did! But then I'd go take an exam and it was like . . . whoa! What the hell is this?! It was like I had never seen this stuff before! Formulas and facts, micros and macros smackin' me in the face and totally blowin' me away. And then suddenly I'm takin' an English exam on Milton's *Paradise Lost*, and all I can think of is Ginger on *Gilligan's Island*. Where's the passion?! Why am I not interested?! I know I'm weird, Newt, but I do not take drugs! Just give me some rock' n' roll!

Okay, here we go. (*Checking the second microphone*) Check. Testing, mic number two. This is Eddie Halley, awake but walkin' in a purple haze. "Jimi Hendrix is dead and gone,"—testing, "but his memory lingers on"—testing. "When his mood was one of bliss,"—testing, "he wrote crushin' tunes like this." (*Playing his air guitar to Hendrix's version of "The Star Spangled Banner"*) De, de, de, de, dede, de dewangg. De, de, de, de, dede, de, dewingg. (*He stops playing and prepares to test the third microphone*) Aaahrightie, let's move on to number three. (*Spotting Newt, who stumbles on the lighting platform*)

Wow, Newt, watch your step up there on that platform. Don't fall, man. (*Reassuringly*) I think I'm gonna like bein' a roadie because, Newt, I see this tour as an educational opportunity to . . . you know . . . learn more about sound . . . power tubes . . . woofers and tweeters, what works and what doesn't. And Louie says he'll give me a few lessons on his axe, teach me a few licks, riffs, some of those funky clean chords, and that chicken-pickin' style he does so well. So I couldn't be happier. And who knows, Newt, maybe I'll find some passion on the road. (*Taking in the future*) Maybe I'll find . . . my sound . . . my voice . . . and then maybe I'll rip through this rock 'n' roll world, out of this stratosphere, find some neoclassical lines, blast some new tunes, and then bring it on home. But for now we're testing number three. (*Speaking into the microphone*)

Mic number three. This is Eddie Halley, testing, rain or shine. "Led Zeppelin, want a whole lotta love,"—testing, "with their throbbing tremolo and fat tone control"— testing. "Brother, they were not foolin',"—testing, "when they sent us back to schoolin'." (*Playing his air guitar to "Whole Lotta Love"*) "Da, Da, dada, Dunt, Dunt, Dunt. Da, Da, dada, Dunt, Dunt, Dunt."

End of Scene

THE BIG BANG

Scene

A recital hall. Selected as members of the state orchestra, the young musicians are about to begin a warm-up exercise before the performance. Thurston, a free-spirited drummer, is one of several percussionists asked to participate in the concert. Even though his instrument is the drum, Thurston was asked to play the gong, which he believes is beneath his level of accomplishment. His friend, confidant, and fellow percussionist, Newton, plays the triangle.

THURSTON: (*Standing next to the gong*) Why did I agree to do this, Newton? I mean, look at all these music geeks—flutes, cellos, violas. This orchestra stuff is too weird. You know me, Newt, I'm strictly rock 'n' roll. I feel like I should take off my shirt when I play the skins; instead I'm standing here in a penguin suit . . . waiting for the conductor-man to point at me so that I can smash this gong with a mallet. (*Amused*) Hey, and look at you, dude. They've got you dingin' a little triangle. Dinga, dinga, dinga. Isn't that precious? You know, I thought people only wore tuxedos at weddings or to the Oscars, or, you know, when they crowned a new president, that kind of thing. But this is tight-ass music, I mean, "bottle up that fart, man, cause it isn't getting' out tonight" kind of music.

(*Pointing out the conductor*) Hey, and did you catch the conductor, know what I mean? That dude is serious. I hear he's from England—some music conservatory. (*Gestures toward the other percussionist*) And look, Newton, look at the Waldo playing the kettle drum . . . the timpani. Man, he looks like he can barely lift those sticks. He must weigh in at about sixty-five pounds. He should be dingin' the triangle, you should be bangin' this gong, and I should be rippin' on the skins. I know it's supposed to be an honor . . . state orchestra . . . all that . . . but it's weird. Can't wait till it's over. (*Sizing up the situation*)

And why do we have to stand way back here, where no one can see us? We should be in the middle, and all these musical yahoos should surround us. The most important sound, percussion, should take center stage, Newton. Am I right? I'm goin' to complain to the conductor. (*Starts to call out*) Hey, Maestro! (*To Newton*) Too late. He's liftin' his little stick. Here we go, Newton. Rock 'n' roll. (*Somewhat surprised*) Hey, he's pointin' to Waldo. Let me see the music. (*Checking out the score*) What do you know, Newton, this piece begins with a drum solo. I guess Waldo is center stage. (*To the other percussionist*) Go get 'em, dude. Be careful; don't hit yourself in the eye. Watch, Newton. He's going to drop a mallet on his first lick. (*The percussionist begins*)

Whoa! That was quite a whack. (*To Newton*) Man, did you see how he put all his weight into that thing. Now, that was cool. Okay. He's workin' the outer edge, yeah. His right hand is talking to his left . . . spirit-like, good, you know, like he's searchin' the softer voices of the drum. (*Impressed*) The kid's got chops . . . some fancy trick-work . . . nice rolls, and some quick waggles with those sticks. (*Growing awareness*) Man, this place is shakin' in here. He's got that skin buzzin' like a beehive . . . and we are vibrating. (*Amazed at the drummer's skill*)

Whoa! Whoa! That was some stroke! (*Barely able to keep his voice down*) Did you hear that, Newton? It's like he grabbed that last lick by the tail, like that note was down deep in a cave somewhere, and he pulled it out fightin' all the way to daylight . . . roarin'! This kid is possessed, man! (*Beginning to lose control*) He's a demon! In battle! Listen to that rhythm, Newton! I've never heard anything like it! (*Becoming more and more vocal—completely involved*) It's primal! Intense! Beautiful. And it's buildin' and buildin' . . . and his hands . . . are flyin' . . . against time! He's hooked into something primal! And we are all like human sacrifices, Newton, and he's drownin' out our cries with the thunderous roar of his drum! (*He roars*) Roarrrrrrrr! (*Silence*) What happened? (*Self-consciously*) Why did he stop? (*Leaning toward the conductor*) What, Maestro? Oh. You want me to hit the gong now. Oh . . . okay. (*He smashes the gong*)

End of Scene

THE PIANO TUNER

Scene

An empty stage, with the exception of maybe a piano tucked into the corner. Tony, a young man in his early twenties, with toolbox in hand, makes his way cautiously to the edge of the stage, which is bathed in white light. Tony is a piano tuner from Brooklyn, and the sound of his voice echoes in the empty theater.

TONY: (*Directing his voice to the top of the theater*) The piano is tuned. Hey, did ya hear me? I tuned that piano. It's ready. (*He listens*) Anyone out there? Hey, can you hear me? Umm, Newt, you up there on the catwalk? You up there? (*Squinting to see beyond the stage lights*) Yeah, you're there, ain't ya? I can hardly see ya under these stage lights. They're too bright. Wave your hand or something. What've you got in your mouth? Is that a rope? A cable? Or what? You focusing lights? (*Nodding*) For the auditions this afternoon? (*Shaking his head*)

I could never perform up here, Newt. On the stage. Under these lights. Under these conditions. (*Placing his toolbox on the stage*) I don't know how they do it. I mean, it makes me nervous just standing here talking to you. I could never audition for people. Honest to God, it makes my stomach bounce just saying the word "audition." But my sister, Theresa, Newt, she was a triple threat . . . though . . . I mean she could sing, dance, act . . . she did it all. Honest to God. I don't know why some Broadway agent didn't scoop her up. I mean, she was an artist . . . a real triple threat. (*Changing the subject*)

Okay, the piano is ready, Newt. If they move it too much, I should have to tune it again. And I . . . ahh . . . located the reason for that vibration. We call it . . . ahh . . . "sympathetic rattle" in the tuning profession. She ain't cracked, thank God, or split, or anything like that. It was a piece . . . of . . . candy . . . or a wad of bubble gum . . . under the soundboard. Can you believe that, Newt? (*Reaching into his toolbox*) And I got the candy out with this piece of hickory stick. Honest to God, I don't understand why anyone would treat a work of art . . . this instrument of the gods . . . like that . . . by throwing a wad of disgusting gum garbage in it! (*With growing irritation*) To me, it's like someone defacing the face of Mona Lisa or carving his initials in the Vietnam Veterans Memorial. They don't deserve to touch it or even be near it. What is it with these people? Don't they know, Newt, that art is rare . . . like the best of our dreams . . . Newt, like my sister, Theresa, the triple threat, who would have loved to audition here . . . but . . . is . . . no longer. Honest to God, Newt, if we are ever to know heaven here on earth, we must take care of the artist and . . . and . . . her instrument. (*He pauses*)

I'm sorry, Newt. I didn't mean to preach to you. I know it's not your fault. I . . . ahh . . . guess . . . I'm feeling a little . . . ahh . . . I don't know . . . emotional . . . today. On this stage. (*Nodding his head*) Well, yeah, I guess auditions start soon . . . uh . . . so . . . ahh . . . you light them well, Newt. You make their faces shine bright. And I hope all these kids auditioning here this afternoon find work. I hope they all get to sing and act and dance. And I'd consider it a privilege to tune their pianos on Broadway . . . some day . . . or even next door at the little theater. (*Collecting his tools*)

So, anyway, you tell 'em that that piano has great action, she's in first-class condition. I've . . . ahh . . . set the temperament . . . and . . . ahh . . . if they treat her well, she will play. And . . . about . . . my sister, Theresa. I hope . . . I just hope, Newt, that some of those characters . . . you know . . . from *Cats, Rent, Little Shop of Horrors, Jesus Christ Superstar,* and all those Rogers and Hammerstein musicals ... well ... I just hope they are in heaven. Otherwise, honest to God, my sister, Theresa, is not very happy. (*He starts to leave*) Oh, yeah, I left the bill on the piano. They need to pay it in ten days.

End of Scene

6

ONE-MINUTE
MONOLOGS FOR
WOMEN

from BIRTH OF A STAR

Scene

An ice-skating rink. A girl delivering a flower arrangement talks to a lone skater on the ice.

PRINCESS IPIA: (*Placing the flowers on the floor*) These are for Julie Snow . . . you know, the amazing skater with the Ice Capades? (*Barely able to contain her joy*) They are a "break a leg" from an admirer. I don't know, do you say "break a leg" to an ice skater? (*With growing excitement*) We come every year, but it seems I've been waiting a long time for this one. I bought my tickets two months ago. (*Locating her seat*) I'm right there: Row J, for Julie, Seat 19, which happens to be how old I am today, nineteen, and I might add that the nineteenth letter in the alphabet is "S" for Snow, and so I guess you can see that I'm just a little bit excited. Ohh. (*Slight laughter*) And my dad has the seat next to me, 20, on the aisle. Julie Snow reminds Dad of my mother. (*Proudly*) My mom was a competitive skater in her twenties, but a knee injury ended all of that. Ohhh. (*Enjoying the reminiscence*) My dad said he fell in love with mother the first time he saw her on the ice . . . figure skating. He used to say, "Princess Ipia"—that's what he calls me—"you could search the universe inside and out, and you would never see anything more beautiful than your mother on skates. She was air and grace, a beautiful blur in motion," he said. And the first time he saw her pirouette and then begin to twirl . . . like they do . . . spinning faster and faster and faster, tucking her arms, collapsing in on herself, he thought he was watching the . . . birth of a star. (*Pauses*) My mother. (*Smiling*) Did I tell you she looked just like Julie Snow?

End of Scene

from BON VOYAGE

Scene

A public beach. Alissa, a lifeguard, talks to her friend about trip to Paris.

ALISSA: (*She blows her whistle*) Hey! You've gone too far. Hey! (*Shouting*) You can't go past the red buoys. (*To her friend nearby*) Hannah, are you packed? I'm just so excited I've been packed for a week. It's the dream of my life. To travel, to Paris, France, on the continent of Europe. Hey! (*She whistles*) I know you can hear this whistle! (*She blows*) So, just put it in reverse, Captain! (*To Hannah*) I've been practicing my French. It gets pretty bad out here watching fat kids bob up and down. They're all sea monsters. Especially that one. (*To the swimmer*) Get on this side of the red buoys! (*To Hannah*) All morning I've been working on *les parties du corps*, "the parts of my body." (*She points to her hair:*) *les cheveux*, (*her nose*) *le nez*, (*her waist*) *la taille*, (*her leg*) *la jambe*, (*her foot*) *le pied*, (*her thumb*) *le pouce*. *Ce va bien, non?* I'm so excited. I can't wait to speak a foreign language in a foreign country and order chicken. (*Blowing her whistle*) That does it! Out of the water! Hannah, do you know who that is out there? Wait a minute. Where's Newton?! I don't see him . . . so it must be . . . Newton! (*Picking up a megaphone*) I know it's you, Newton. Just paddle your fanny back to shore. I'm going to count to three and then I'm calling the authorities. *Un!* Turn around, Newton. *Deux!* I will not swim out there! I'm off duty in two minutes, my hair is dry, my back is peeling, and I'm going to Paris tomorrow! *Trois!* Okay, go ahead. Sail away. *Au revoir*, idiot, *bon voyage* and see if I care. (*She throws up her middle finger*) *Le doight*, dork! (*To Hannah*) Hannah, are you taking a hairdryer?

End of Scene

Chapter 6

from HOOFER

Scene

A few scattered chairs and maybe a piano are found on what is otherwise an empty stage.

ZENITH BLACKETER: (*Rhythmically, she sings*) Be-dee-bop, be-dee-bop, be-dee-bop! (*Catching her breath*) Whew! I'm feeling a little lightheaded. I didn't eat before I came here. Did you? I don't like to dance on a full stomach. Since my audition's at two, I thought I could make it through. But I don't know. (*Singing*) Be-dee-dee-bop, Be-dee-bop! Be-dee-bop! That's just one of my little warm-ups. I need to sing the rhythm before I tap it. Oh, Newton, I hate to audition. It's so hard. And I already know the outcome. (*Reeling from insecurity*) She won't cast me; I just know it. And I know what she's thinking. (*With growing anxiety*) I'm not the right . . . size . . . my thighs are too big or they're too small . . . I'm too tall . . . or short. I don't have the right name . . . or . . . religion . . . or birthdate . . . or zip code . . . or sexual orientation . . . or parents . . . or maybe she's still angry with me because of that damn stupid production of *Oklahoma!* (*A loud confession*) I didn't mean to kick Curly in the head during final dress, Newton. It was an accident! I'm a hoofer, for crying out loud, Newton! And a hoofer moves! (*Her emotions are spilling over*) No. I will walk on stage (*Demonstrating*), say my name . . . "Zenith Blacketer" . . . and before I finish saying, "This afternoon I am dancing to a tap classic, 'Sweet Georgia Brown,'" she'll say, "Next!" She'll never see me tap! Well, that's just too bad. It is her loss! I'm part of an American institution, Newton. I am Ruby Keeler and Shirley Temple, rolled into one . . . I am Zenith Blacketer . . . and I have tap in my blood. Loud and snappy! (*Singing and tapping with excess emotion*) Spank! Spank! Dee-dee-dee-Dee-Bop!

End of Scene

from TRACTORS AND TWIRLERS

Scene

A sidewalk on Main Street during the annual Thanksgiving parade.

JULIE STALBIRD: (*A ringing endorsement*) I love a parade. (*To Newton*) My dad said a parade "is top-choice America." And he thinks the Thanksgiving Parade is "America cut thick and prime." (*Laughing*) Well, I don't know about that, Newton, but I do love a parade. (*Spotting a friend*) Oh, wouldn't you know, here comes the Pork Queen, Rita—Rita Wright. (*Calling out*) Hi, Rita! You look beautiful! And nice hair, too. (*Confiding to Newton*) Do you know Rita, Newton? Well, she's nice enough, but she's no Pork Queen. It's all who you know, you know. Her father owns Wright Farm. (*Shocked and near the point of tears*) Oh, no, here they come, Newton, the Twirlers. I'm not sure I can stand it. Daddy told me I would have to face this sooner or later . . . but I just hurt so much and I'm still so angry. (*Sitting down*) I'm going to sit down right here, grip the curb, and try my best to keep from bursting. (*Almost hysterical*) Oh, God. Look at them . . . twirl. I twirled for eight years, Newton. And then . . . this . . . Mrs. Troutman took over the Twirlers and cut me from the team. She cut me deep, Newton. And it's not fair! I should lead . . . the Twirlers . . . and . . . I just can't stand it . . . anymore! It's just not fair! (*Shouting out*) Mrs. Troutman . . . you are a fascist! A Martha Stewart wannabe! You and your perfect squad . . . of size-six twirlers . . . all looking very . . . slim . . . and very . . . much . . . alike! This is America, Mrs. Troutman! We . . . welcome . . . diversity! (*Sighing*) There. (*Collecting herself*) I feel better now. I just had to fling that thing up into the air and just let it twirl away. And I'm not ashamed, Newton, because I want Mrs. Troutman and all of her little Twirlers to feel my pain. Happy Thanksgiving. There. Yes, I feel much better now. (*Sighs*) I love a parade.

End of Scene

from ODE TO LITTLE AUDREY

Scene

A sidewalk near a city street. Audrey, a young girl, is jumping rope with a friend.

AUDREY: "Oxen free!" (*Jumping rope and reciting*)
"Tick tock, the game is locked,
Nobody else can play.
And if they do, we'll take their shoe
And we'll beat them black and blue (and purple too!)"

(*Stops jumping—showing mild irritation*) What is the matter with you, Newton? When I say "oxen free," it means you can move. So stand up and get ready to jump. You know, I believe you are walking around in a turkey's dream! (*Looking down the street, she studies the approaching caravan of cars*) Oh . . . here they come. And look, they all have their headlights on, Newton, and the policeman is waving them through the stop sign. Which car is she in? The first or the second? (*Nodding*) First. And your family is in the second. Hmmm. (*Noticing*) The car has stopped, Newton, and I guess it's time to jump to Grandma's rhyme. Ready. Here we go.
(*Jumping rope and reciting*)

"Down in the valley
Where the green grass grow
There sat Grandma
Sweet as a rose
She sang, she sang,
She sang so sweet;
Along came Grandpa
And kissed her on the cheek.
How many kisses did she get that day?
One, two, three, four . . ."

(*They stop skipping and watch the car pass by. Audrey begins to laugh*) You know, Newton, your Grandmother was a pretty good rope-jumper, too, until she broke her hip. But you must get your talent for jumping rope from your Grandfather's side of the family, because you jump rope like a rooster in mud. (*Skipping off and reciting*)

"Charlie Chaplin went to France
To teach the ladies how to dance;
First the heel and then the toe,
A skip and a hop and away you go!"

End of Scene

from HUMMERS, ROCKETS, AND SPLIT COMETS

Scene

A clear summer night on the Fourth of July. Shelley reaches a landing on the rugged hillside to the watch the city fireworks.

SHELLEY: (*Excited and reaching skyward*) There it is! Just waiting for someone to paint it. Like a backdrop, a canvas primed and stretched tight. What a beautiful night! (*Calling down to Newton*) Hurry up, Newton! You're going to miss the finale! I love those hummers, rockets, and split comets. (*Imitating the sound of fireworks*) Pa-boom! Pop! Pop! Pa-boom! (*Pleasantly startled*) Wow! Did you see that? This place is perfect! Just like in the movies . . . perfect! (*Echoing the sound*) Pa-boom! Pop! Pop! Ka-boom! Hurry, Newton! The finale is almost here. And I want it to be just like that old movie we watched. You, Newton, will be Cary Grant and, I, Shelley, will be Grace Kelly, and the fireworks will be the fireworks, so . . . pull yourself up here Newton! *Ka-boom!* That was incredible! It was like a blooming white flower filling the sky. And when it seemed like it was over, and the last of the petals began to fade, green frogs began leaping in all directions, landing on the bellies of surprised water snakes, who, spitting and fizzing, whipped about, flinging sparks, helter-skelter into the night sky. It was amazing, Newton! And I want it to happen again and again! *Ka-boom! Ka-boom*! Newton, it's the finale! *Ka-boom*! I just want to reach up and grab this wonderful night! (*She reaches upward*) Or maybe you, Newton. My Cary Grant, hurry! On a night light this, with a sky like that, anything is possible. That's right, Newton, anything! (*Silence. She listens*) Well. Hmmm . . . I guess it's over. Ahhh . . . well . . . I guess you missed the finale, Newton. It certainly was a beautiful sight. (*Sighs, nonchalantly*) Well, who knows, maybe you will make it next year. I'm coming down now, Newton. I'm coming down.

End of Scene

from **F = W**D

Scene

A college dorm room. Sarah vents her anger about dorm life.

SARAH: (*Stepping into her room*) Did you hear what happened out there, Ruthie? I knocked on Newton's door and asked if I could borrow a pencil ... to do my math ... and then his girlfriend ... the frigging Frog Lady ... leaps out into the hall and croaks, "I know what you're thinking!" And so I yell back, "You do? Okay, tell me: When does the formula $F = Wd$ not apply?" To which she answered, "His pencil!" Jesus, Ruthie, psych majors! They see the whole world through Freudian sunglasses. I've had it up to here with the fruitcakes on this floor and especially the Frog Lady, so I took off on her, Ruthie. "You're wrong, Frog Lady! (*Building up steam*) Think about the formula this way. You are a *constant force* to deal with ... see ... so Frog-lady equals F, which stands for *force*. Now you weigh, I'd say, in that neighborhood of about ... one hundred and sixty pounds, more or more. And you're trying your damnedest to throw your saturated beef around, see, pushing me just ten feet down the hall ... here. So, in this example, the work done is ten times one hundred sixty, or 1,600 foot-pounds. So, Frog Lady, if you are knocked on your ass ... say ... by a sleep-deprived science major ... me ... before you push her ... me ... ten feet, the formula $W = Fd$ does not apply! (*Feeling pleased with herself*) Well, Ruthie, I think that was an educated response, don't you? Suddenly, I found some real application of the study of differential calculus. (*Changing the subject*) Do you want to order a pizza?

End of Scene

from STAGE FRIGHT PIANOLOGUE

Scene

A recital hall. A piano accompanist, Nicole, enters hurriedly from the wings.

NICOLE: (*Wringing her hands*) I'm ah . . . the accompanist. (*Checking a wristwatch*) Am I late? No. Good. (*Makes her way to the piano*) Okay. Well . . . I'm sorry if I seem a little shaky. I work with singers in practice rooms, but not in public. So I'm just a little bit nervous, standing . . . here . . . here . . . on the . . . ah . . . stage. (*Begins to shake*) I have a . . . ah . . . little stage fright . . . theatrophobia. (*Nervous laughter*) Hehehe! But . . . ah . . . I'll be all right. Whew! Say . . . how . . . how many people does this theater seat? Ohhh. (*Overwhelmed*) About four . . . four hundred. Whew! Okay . . . and the singers are auditioning for light operas . . . Gilbert and Sullivan . . . right? (*Trying to be positive*) Ohh . . . good . . . some of my favorites . . . (*Failing*) well, not really . . . sometimes all that bantering . . . all that wordplay . . . you know . . . makes me a little nervous. (*Fearfully*) They're not going to recite poetry, are they? Oh, great. It's just that my doctor thinks I have a little fear of poetry . . . metrophobia . . . with a just a . . . a slight touch of . . . a . . . verbaphobia . . . a fear . . . of . . . of . . . words . . . but . . . I'll be fine as long as you don't ask me to recite anything. Breathe! (*She does*) Wow! That was a dry mouthful. (*She laughs*) Hehehe. I feel better now. (*On the verge of exploding*) You know, this is a big room. Whew! (*Mounting anxiety*) It's high and wide and deep . . . and . . . and I think I'm fine with it . . . except my throat is tightening . . . just a little. I mean, that last session with my doctor in that abandoned warehouse . . . ah . . . basically . . . purged my fear of kenophobia . . . large, empty spaces. But this isn't really an empty space . . . it's a theater . . . hehehe . . . which . . . I believe

I told you . . . makes me a little bit nervous . . . nauseous . . . maybe it's because the theater contains all of my fears: theatro, glosso, halo, keno, metro, verba . . . and probably the worst . . . being stared at . . . opthalmophobia . . . like right now . . . by you! (*Her anxiety peaks—almost hysterical*) It is hot in here. Very hot. I can't breath. Nauseous. Very nauseous. And I need a drink of water. I've got to go . . . get some . . . (*A speedy exit*)

End of Scene

from BUCKAROO BELLE AND THE BULL RIDER

Scene

A rodeo. Katie Belle, a bull-riding instructor, coaches a newcomer to the sport of competitive bull riding.

KATIE BELLE: (*Excitedly*) Just eight seconds, Newton. Yee-hahh! Just eight tiny ticks of the clock, and it's all over. But first we're gonna do a little warm-up exercise. So climb up there on that barrel. I'll ride along side you. (*Mounting a barrel*) You'll be riding Starburst. He's bucked fifteen riders, but I think he's ready to give it up to the right man. I think you're the one. But first, I want you to visualize a perfect ride up here on these barrels. Here we go. Just relax. Good. Smell the bull. (*Takes a deep breath*) Hmm . . . he smells good, don't he? (*Going through the motions*) Now, grip the leather rope in your hand and lift your free hand way back—ready to slice the air. Relaxed and balanced, just sittin' on top of old Starburst, we're gonna take a little ride. Now, I want you to imagine something beautiful, like biscuits and butter, or maybe me, Katie Belle. Once that vision is planted in your head, I'll give the word, the chute gate will open, and you will . . . (*Distracted by a rider*) Hey, look-a there, Newton. It's your friend. Ol' Hurley. He's riding Diablo. That bull is one mean six-year-old. (*Calling out*) Go get him, Hurley! (*To Newton*) He's quick . . . just watch how he explodes out of the chute. He'll make a couple jumps, and then there's a ninety percent chance he'll spin, like a whirl-a-gig, to the right. (*Cheering*) Go get him, Hurley. (*Broadcasting*) Gates opened. Whoa! Hang on, Hurley! Hang on! Don't panic! He's going to his left, Hurley! Watch it! Wow! (*The rider is tossed*) Lift off! He's flying! All four feet off the ground! Get out of there, Hurley! That was some ride! (*With great fanfare*) Yee-hahh! That bull exploded! I mean, just three seconds in . . . Diablo came to a complete stop . . . then he launched into the air just like a rocket! Like he was defying gravity! And ol' Hurley . . . was just tossed on his head . . . like he was nothing! Now, that was excitement. That was a ride! (*Calling out*) Hey, foreman, I want to ride old Diablo. Sign me up!

End of Scene

from CHOCOLATE THIN MINTS

Scene
A college. Virginia, a first-year college student, enters the office of the Director of Residential Life.

VIRGINIA DARE: (*Forcefully*) Are you the Director of Residential Life? Good. I need to talk to you about roommate assignments? Mine isn't working out. Irreconcilable differences. It's time for a divorce. My name is Virginia. Virginia Dare . . . just like the first-born child in the New World. (*Making sure he understands*) My roommate's name is Lilith Cain. We've been roommates now for almost a whole semester. I didn't know Lilith before I came to school here. She's from the North and I'm from the South . . . and, well . . . I was naturally just a tad apprehensive, but I love this school and I want to honor that part in our preamble that states: "Each student is a bright piece of glass in our cultural mosaic." I appreciate that. (*Sincerely*) I do. It's just that, I don't understand her speech, and that's a problem because she talks nonstop. (*A quick breath*) Another thing, between you and me, I think she's too skinny. (*Feigning confidentiality*) And I don't want to spread rumors, and so I hope that I'm wrong, but she might be bulimic. Lord have mercy. (*Amazed*) I mean, she eats a lot, but I don't know where it goes. She has a full meal plan, one of those compact refrigerators . . . stuffed, and the top drawer of her dresser is layered with boxes of Girl Scout cookies, chocolate Thin Mints, my favorite. The way that girl eats, she should weigh more than my Uncle Willie's prize heifer. But, I think she's a size two. That's not much of an exaggeration. (*Knowingly*) I guess it's her metabolism. Or maybe she's just throwing it all up. Whatever, it's not fair. (*A confession*) I battle my weight constantly. From day one, Lilith has been highly critical of me. You should see the expression on her face if I have just a tiny snack between meals. Well, I'm tired of that! I mean, I enrolled in college, not a fat camp. I don't want a skinny roommate any longer. (*Decisively*) So, Mr. Director of Residential Life, we need to check your files for a few good candidates.

End of Scene

Chapter 6

from THE TWILIGHT ARCH

Scene
*An open field. Two young college students have climbed a ridge
to listen for the howling of coyotes.*

TORRIE: This is the spot. This is the best place in the county to
hear them. (*Sitting*) I know some kids go over to Reuben's Ridge,
but I like this place, this hill. (*Removing her shoes*) It's like a natural outdoor theater or something. And look at the stars. How
bright! How they light up the sky! Professor Andersen has
a bumper sticker on his truck. Have you seen it? It's crazy, it says,
"Light speed. 185,000 miles per second. It's the law." He's a
character. (*She laughs*) He makes me laugh. (*Slight pause*) Look!
(*Pointing*) There it is. Just like the professor told us. What did he
call it? The arch. Yes, the twilight arch—you see, there, a pink
band of color in the sky with the dark area underneath. It's the
Earth casting its shadow on our atmosphere. You see it, don't
you? It's amazing! And a little bit ominous. We are so lucky to be
here. Under the sky. (*She rises*) They will start soon. Oh, I love to
hear them. Sometimes, when I'm bored or trapped by school
or home or friends, I think of the coyotes . . . out here . . .
roaming the land . . . free . . . and howling. The sound digs
deep, and it makes me feel good, right here inside, to hear the cry
of the coyotes. They make me smile. Look, I've made you smile.
Your eyes are very expressive. You know, I feel like I can trust
you . . . with a secret. It's because your eyes are very honest. And
I want to be honest, too. (*Coyotes howl*) Shhh. There. Listen.
(*Excitedly*) They are howling. Howling. Isn't it beautiful! Isn't it
the most beautiful sound you've ever heard? (*A forceful whisper*)
Aaaooohh! Aaaooohhh! Come on, we should join in their song.
(*She begins to howl*) Aaaoooohh! Aaaooooohh! (*Encouraging*) Howl,
howl. It will make you laugh.

End of Scene

from LIZZIE'S LILLIPUT

Scene

Lizzie, a college student, shares her "week of silence" experience with a friend.

LIZZIE: I didn't always behave this way, this grown-up, this mature. For a while I was a bleached blond boxie, a glitter-bag, and then a bizotic, i.e., bizarre plus exotic equals weird, and then finally, a brainiac. As you might guess, there were many bumps in the road on the way to finding my intelligence, I used to talk like, "Duh," "You know," "I mean," like a Val girl, and then one day my speech teacher, Mr. Bell, dropped a bomb in class. Ka-boom! He quoted Jonathan Swift, the guy who wrote *Gulliver's Travels*, who said, ". . . every word we speak is in some degree a diminution of our lungs by corrosion, and consequently contributes to the shortening of our lives." (*Reliving the shock*) "Oh, God!" I thought. "This is horrible! Why didn't someone tell me before?" You see, throughout my adolescent years, I was an habitual talker, a blabberer who never shut her mouth. And although I was only fifteen at the time I learned about this talking disease, I figured in terms of the number of words I had spoken in my life, I was probably closer to sixty-five or seventy. And so, I had to quit immediately. (*A painful memory*) For a whole week I didn't say a word. Not one utterance. It was very painful . . . and it made me really stressed and nervous . . . and at times I could hardly breathe. And let me tell you, all through that week I had uncontrollable urges to talk . . . to say just one word . . . to express . . . or to affirm . . . with just one word. But I stayed strong and resisted. For that whole week, I remained silent. It was very awkward. I didn't know how to explain to my friends that talking was sending me prematurely to the grave, and I didn't want them to think that I had become a "Waldo," and so I wore a sign on my sweater: "I am remaining silent to protest world hunger." It was the most difficult week of my life.

End of Scene

from Two Blushing Pilgrims

Scene

A theater. Kari, a costume and makeup assistant, enters carrying supplies.

KARI: (*To the stage manager*) Open the dressing rooms. I've got to make moustaches and bald caps for those pubescent friars . . . and . . . a . . . "But soft! What light through yonder window breaks?" Our chubby little Romeo split his pants again. Actors. (*Rattling off issues*) Juliet's having her period; she hates her parents, is thinking about getting an apartment. Mercutio is coming out of the closet tonight, before the curtain, at the company meeting. I said, "No, Mercutio, the director wouldn't like that. Save it for the cast party." He tells me, "Kari, I can't wait another minute because I'm sick of living a lie. Besides," he says, "it will free my emotions and liberate my acting." So, stay tuned tonight; Mercutio will give new meaning to his line: "Here's my fiddlestick; here's that shall make you dance." Thank God theater isn't, in *stricta sensu*, a science. This place would explode like the bull's eye on a test site in Nevada. (*Building her vision*) The thing is, you've got all this emotion running wild backstage before the show. And as each actor arrives and signs his name to the callboard, he tosses in more emotion. (*Rapidly*) So they're all running around looking for me or for anyone who will listen, and their heads are popping off, and their pants are ripped, they are not gay but are gay, and they're pissed off at each other, their mothers and lovers, and they're crying, and their makeup runs, and their shoes don't fit, and there is not a tampon to be found anywhere! (*Breathes*) It's chaos. Not one tampon. Theater backstage is human life *in extremis*. (*Sudden pleasantness*) And then, you show up. Our stage manager. And you say, "Places." With such authority. And suddenly, they all shut up. Suddenly, all that confusion and chaos is gone as they whisper "break a leg" and hug each other, because now there is order. You see, they are working together to make something beautiful . . . or . . . maybe . . . they're just in that state of shock . . . you know, like a deer caught in headlights. (*Smiling*) Which is the way I felt last night, with you. Shockingly beautiful and just a little naughty.

End of Scene

from HARD KNOCKS

Scene

A stage. Darcy introduces actors auditioning for the title role of
Annie, *while also talking to the musical director.*

DARCY WELLS: (*To a child actor*) That's right. Smile! Good.
Next! (*To the director seated in the theater, loudly*) Her number is
fourteen! (*To Sandy, who is at the foot of the stage*) It's in my
blood. My grandmother attended the Hamilton School
of Dramatic Expression. I get my talent from her side of the
family. (*To another child actor*) Okay, next! Center stage and
smile, Angel! Show them your teeth and plenty of 'em. Okay,
Angel? You can move back now. Get back in line. Next! Smile!
That's good. (*To the director*) Number sixteen. (*To Sandy*) They
insisted that I take this job helping the director, Sandy,
because, and it is not easy for me to say this, they did not want
me to audition. I know it. And I know they know I know it.
(*To a child actor*) Is that your real hair? (*To the director*) She says
it's her real hair. Isn't it cute? (*To the actor*) You can go back
now. Next! (*To Sandy*) I was the first Annie to perform at
the Firehouse Theater. Did you see it? Too bad. I have a
mid-belty voice and when I sang, (*Singing with some restraint*)
"Tomorrow, tomorrow, I love ya, tomorrow. You're only a day
away," the audience went wild. But when they revived it the
next year, a younger girl replaced me. In just one year, I guess
I had gotten too old for the role. Actually, it wasn't my voice,
it was my feet. They had grown rather large in a very short
period of time . . . and backstage at the auditions . . . I overheard Daddy Warbucks tell the costumer that my tapping
sounded more like . . . clogging. (*Showing some pain*) So in just
a few months, I went from the title role to one of the mutts in
the orphanage. Watch your back, Sandy. You cannot trust
anyone in show business. Especially Daddy Warbucks. And

I thought he was such a great man. (*To a child actor*) Smile, honey, lift your chin and smile! "You're never fully dressed without a smile."

End of Scene

from HEAD SHOTS AND HOT BUTTERED BISCUITS (MONOLOG ONE)

Scene

An empty stage. Charlotta, a newcomer to the stage, seeks help as she prepares for an audition.

CHARLOTTA: (*Addressing a director, seated in the theater*) What do you think of my head shot? (*Holding up her résumé*) Do I need a new eight-by-ten? You've got to have a great photo in this business. It's, like, the first thing they see, you know, unless, of course, you know someone, and then it doesn't matter. (*A deep breath*) But I don't know anyone in the business. Well, except you, and . . . uh . . . you're not exactly Oprah Winfrey, now are you? Just kidding about that. (*She breathes*) I just think it might be too glossy, you know what I mean? I asked the photographer to touch up that scar over my right eye, but he said no, it gives me character, you know, like Marilyn Monroe's mole. I said, "I don't want character; I want beauty." Now I'm stuck with fifty of these eight-by-tens. Ouch! Well, hell's bells, but if you can keep a secret (*Ensuring their privacy*), I might have a little P.S.— (*Whispering*) plastic surgery—to remove that scar before I start a film career, which I plan to do . . . any day now. And maybe while I'm at it . . . I'll tighten up the booty. But I'm not real comfortable with that idea just yet because just yesterday I read about this lady who asked her surgeon to add shape to her butt . . . which I guess they can do now. Anyway, it seems he used those silicone breast implants, planted one in each cheek, and now . . . ouch . . . she's got boobs on her butt! Let me repeat that: boobs on her butt! She's sporting two pair: one upstairs and one on her derrière. I imagine she's just a little bit angry and her boyfriend is a little bit overwhelmed. So I'm thinking I'll wait a while on the butt surgery. It's not too bad, is it? My butt? (*Showing it off, and noticing embarrassment*) I believe you are turning red. Yes. Well, what do you know? You are blushing! I believe I have embarrassed you, talking about my body parts. I must have stimulated your little red head. Who would have guessed? (*Laughing*) Forgive me. I don't mean to laugh. Please. (*Drawing breath*) Back to business.

End of Scene

from HEAD SHOTS AND HOT BUTTERED BISCUITS (MONOLOG TWO)

Scene

An empty stage. Charlotta, a newcomer to the stage, seeks help as she prepares for an audition.

CHARLOTTA: Did you look at the backside of my résumé? (*Turning her résumé over*) I didn't know how much information to include. I want them to know that I'm not a beginner. Right? (*Proudly*) And as you can see, for two whole years I was the Decapitated Princess, Stella, in Dr. Magic's Show of Optical Tricks. It was called the "Tavern of the Dead," and it was a lot of fun until Dr. Magic decided to expand his act to include sword swallowing and knife throwing. There, at the bottom of the page, someone told me to list my special skills, which, I admit, are limited, and so, as you can see, I've included Hula-Hoop trickster and horseback rider. Well, I am an expert Hula-Hooper, but between you and me, I've never been on a horse. I did ride an elephant for a whole season with Winky's Little Top Circus and it was a lot of fun, but I believe all that jostling caused me to have irregular periods, and I lost all interest in dating. But I didn't fall off, and so I figured, if I can ride one four-legged beast, I could wrap my legs around any of them. Whoops! (*Suppressing laughter*) That didn't sound very nice, did it? If you don't shut me up, I'll talk until doomsday, and I just might say something I'll regret . . . and embarrass us both. So, on with the show. (*A deep breath, a few steps to center stage. She begins her audition*) My name . . . oh . . . I was told I should first announce my name and then announce the piece. (*Seeking confirmation*) Is that right? Just nod your head. Okay, so, here goes. (*Breathing deeply*) My name is Charlotta Corday. (*Whispering*) That's my stage name, by the way. And for my first audition, I am doing Maggie from *Cat on a Hot Tin Roof* by Tennessee Williams. (*A forceful announcement*) "One of those no-neck monsters hit me with a hot buttered biscuit, so I have t' change!" (*Tries to hold her laughter but fails*) Oh, God. I can hardly say that without laughing. (*Stepping toward*) Do you know this play? It is soooo good. You have a nice smile. Are you gay?

End of Scene

from BEAST BALLET

Scene

Renee, an overly confident prima ballerina, is working with a newly recruited Beauty and the Beast *company member.*

RENEE: (*Assuming the proper stance*) First position. Heels together. Feet turned out. More. I know it hurts, but in first position you have to make a single line with your feet. Okay? Out, left foot, out, right foot. Yuck! (*Breaks from the position*) You know, you have a bad case of knock-knee. I mean, honestly, it's a physical defect and it looks extremely unpleasant on a dancer unless you join a company of orangutans. But don't cry about it. Who knows, in a year or two, if you stay in ballet, you just might grow out of it. (*Assumes first position*) Okay, now, *entrechat!* (*Stops before the leap*) Just kidding. Not ready for that yet! We'll concentrate on the five positions only so that we can plant you in the *corps* ... in the forest scene. (*Instructing*) Second position. Keep the feet out. Out, out, I say! Balance ... good ... hold it! (*Stepping around*) Now, I'm going to step in front of you (*Executing the move*) and I'll make the fourth position *efface*, like this, while you stay in second. See. Now we're making a tree. Nothing to it. Now put your hands around my waist. Good ... good God! (*Showing disgust*) Look at the hair on the back of your hands. Yuck! I've never seen so much hair on a person's hands before. You must be still evolving. Okay. (*Executing the move*) Third position. Return to first ... well ... now each heel touches the middle of the opposite foot. Feels good, doesn't it? Hold it, hold it, balance, breathe. You are going to be one stumpy tree, with your short, knotty legs and very long torso ... and so ... sorry to be the messenger ... but you won't be doing a solo any time soon. Oh, but don't you love the third position ... how it just pushes everything up? (*Standing tall*) It forces you to think strong. In control. Like on a launch pad, a powerful whirligig, about to conquer space. I wish we could stay in this position forever . . . but we must move on. (*Instructing*) Fourth position. Right foot out, toe and heel line up . . . good. (*Pauses*) You know, you're not totally unattractive. But you might see a doctor about that hand hair. That's the lesson. Time to go. Go, be a beautiful tree.

End of Scene

7 ONE-MINUTE MONOLOGS FOR MEN

from A LEAN, MEAN, SINGING MACHINE

Scene
A recital hall. Otto barks commands to the Newton Community Chorus.

OTTO GUNTHER: (*Addressing the chorus*) All right, now. All of you. Listen up! I'm Otto Gunther . . . and I'm not here to be your friend. I'm here to make a chorus! A lean, mean, singing machine. We got only four weeks, four weeks, I said, to put the *Messiah* together. So hate me now . . . hate me later . . . but I'm gonna whip the *Messiah* out of you. But before I go on, there are a couple of things you need to know about me . . . Gunther. Firstly, I want you all to know my philosophy. (*Raising his hand*) Do I have any strippers in the chorus? (*Slight pause*) I ask you, do any of you take off your clothes before an audience? I don't mean G-strings and pasties . . . I mean the complete birthday suit . . . triple X, exposed . . . you know, like those monkeys on the Discovery Channel when they rise up and turn their butts to the camera and suddenly you're lookin' at this large, red, meaty . . . pustule. Now that's exposed! That's naked! Hahaha. And that's my philosophy. (*Emphatically*) Singin' before an audience is the same as strippin' before an audience. And so, my little songbirds, if you are ashamed of your . . . pustule . . . this chorus is not the place for you. Hahaha. Hey, I didn't ask to walk upright . . . I was happy being a monkey, but since I'm standin', we might as well sing. All right. (*Waving the music*) This is gonna take some fancy lip and lung action—it's a moody piece . . . one minute you're singin' all happy-like . . . voices are zippin' in and out of there . . . praisin' the glory of the Lord . . . and isn't this pure and bring on the good stuff and then . . . bam! Shit hits the fan! And we're pissed off! And sad! And grievin'! And generally having a hell of a time comin' to grips with this whole Messiah mess . . . until . . . suddenly, suddenly, it all comes together and you can't help but be thrilled and so you sing! And you sing perfect! And in your vocal nakedness . . . you wash the audience with astonishment, as we all rise up and shout (*Singing*), "Hallelujah! Hallelujah! Hallelujah!" (*Stops*) Hey, hey, wait a minute! Bring down the curtain! Shit! I think I left my lights on . . . I'll be back in a minute. (*A quick exit*)

End of Scene

from PETER PAN AND THE SQUARE-RIGGER

Scene

A stage. Joel, an Irish sailor, has volunteered to help with a production of "Peter Pan."

JOEL: (*Searching the catwalks*) Mr. Boker! They said you'd be walking the catwalks, fixing cable, and the like. You know, Captain, when I learned of your plans to fly real people around the stage, I thought, "Wallop me ass with a cannon-ball! Theater people are crazy!" But then I watched the rehearsal of your play, *Peter Pan*, and I began to understand your determination. Just because we are no longer children, it doesn't mean we must give up on our dreams. It's an admirable thing you are doing, Captain. And so, just believe in my crew, and your Peter Pan and the Darlings will fly. (*Interrupted by his crew singing*) One moment, Captain. (*Commanding the crew*) Quiet, you scugs! That's a shitty tune you're singing. Now bring it together, or I'll be getting angry. (*To the technical director*) Sorry, Captain, but no two sailors ever sing the same shanty in quite the same way. Aye, but to do a job right, the boys have to sing and heave ho together. It is a performing art. Much like the theater, I daresay. I had never considered it before, but there is much we have in common: (*Looking around*) stage drapes like sails, ropes, rigging, running lights, and a crew and actors. Aye. (*With admiration*) A salty lot who have a difficult time keeping their feet on dry land . . . who, I imagine, are more at home in the exhilaration of a performance . . . a ship on the open sea. (*Heartfelt*) And so, Captain, if I could wish you one wish, it would be to stand on the polished teak fore-castle of a ship in deep water. A square-rigger with her sails full, like healthy young lungs, from jib to spanker, sails, fore and aft, riding a nor'eastern trade wind, making time, bound to some exotic port. Aye. (*Truthfully*) It is an artful life to be a sailor on a real ship. But I'm sorry to say, there isn't much of a demand . . . for square-rigged . . . sailors. I wish the theater better success. (*Again interrupted by the crew singing*) The tune! The tune! Don't make me ashamed of our performance. If your singing isn't in tune with the others, you will drop that little Peter Pan on her arse.

End of Scene

from A SEAMLESS PITCH

Scene

The beach. Allen and Angela are skipping pebbles along the top of the water.

ALLEN: (*Watching Angela's throw*) Ooh! One, two, three. Three skips, Angela. That's good, but you've got to find the right pebble . . . flat and smooth. (*Locating a pebble*) Wouldn't it be great, Angela, if you could skip a pebble all the way from the shores of America to the shores of Africa . . . to your hometown . . . what is it . . . now, don't tell me . . . I know it. Port Gentil in Gabon. It sounds like an incredible place. And hot! I can't believe you live on the equator . . . zero degrees latitude . . . the equator! It must be scorching! I'm out in the sun five minutes and I look like boiled shrimp! (*Studies her*) But your skin is perfect, and your eyes . . . (*Recalling the past*) I still remember the first day you walked into our class. We were reading a scene from *Romeo and Juliet* . . . the party scene . . . everyone was wearing these construction-paper masks we had made a few minutes earlier. Romeo was describing Juliet to Tybalt . . . and suddenly you appeared in the doorway . . . I don't know . . . like a vision . . . like it was planned or something. And then Romeo said: (*Reciting the speech*)

O, She doth teach the torches to burn bright!
It seems she hangs upon the cheek of night
As a rich jewel in an Ethiop's ear—
Beauty too rich for use, for earth too dear.

You took an empty seat next to me. (*A wash of emotion*) I . . . ahh . . . was afraid to look at you . . . to catch your eye . . . but when I did . . . you smiled. I thought . . . *she likes me.* I was wearing this mask . . . it was kind of a rabbit's face . . . pink ears . . . and buck teeth . . . and it hit me that it might not be me you like ... but the rabbit. So ... I was stuck for the rest of that class, afraid to take off the mask, wondering what you would think if you saw the real me. (*Slight laugh*) That's pretty stupid, isn't it? (*Watching her throw*) Five skips. Great, Angela. Some day, I'm going to visit your country ... and we will stand on the beach at Port Gentil and skip stones toward America.

End of Scene

from THE 1ˢᵀ DEAD MAN IN GROVER'S CORNERS

Scene

A dress rehearsal for "Our Town." The 1ˢᵗ Dead Man steps out of character to chastise the director.

1ˢᵀ DEAD MAN: You know, Ludwig, we open in three nights, and we have not had one complete run-through. It was a mistake casting Newton as George. He's a nitwit! And he's ruining *Our Town*! It's shameful. This is going to be the worst production of *Our Town* in the history of community theater. Hey, I know I'm just the First Dead Man, but I've put a lot of hours into this production, and I think I am speaking for all the dead . . . here. Right, folks? (*Spotting a child in the wings*) Hey! Tycho! Don't touch the counterweight system! Stay away from that electric winch. You're going to drop a full batten of lighting instruments and kill everyone in the graveyard. Tycho! Get away from there! (*To the actor playing Emily, who also happens to be Tycho's mother*) Emily, that kid of yours doesn't need to be running around backstage, making a nuisance of himself. And don't give me that crap about (*Quoting the play*) "People don't understand. And how troubled and dark our lives are." That kid is a nuisance . . . a regular Dennis the Menace . . . and if I catch him in my dressing room again, I'm going to slice off a piece of his nose. What kind of a name is "Tycho" anyway? What is his father? A Lego toy? (*To the director*) Hey, Ludwig, don't you have a rule about outsiders at rehearsal? (*The director leaves the theater*) Hey, where are you going? Are we taking a break? Because if this is a break, I didn't have a chance to eat, and I need some nourishment. I'm not staying in this graveyard any longer . . . this place stinks! (*Turns on everyone*) Aya, you all stink! I'm going down to the green room, and, guess what? I'm making a huge pot of New England clam chowder. Aya. Enough for all. (*Mockingly*) Then we can all sit around the green room table, chat, and sip soup, because in *Our Town*, "We like to know the real facts about everybody in Grover's Corners." For example, is Tycho really a boy, or a devil child? Actors . . . my . . . my, isn't theater awful—and wonderful? I'll be in the green room if you want me.

End of Scene

from DODGEBALL MATADOR

Scene
High-school P.E. class. Adam is forced to play dodgeball.

ADAM: Whoa! That was close. (*To his friend*) I hate this game. I'm going to get donked any minute now. I feel like Piggy in *Lord of the Flies*! After all these years of school, higher math, language studies, and years of Spanish, my diploma now depends on my ability to dodge a ball. It isn't fair! This is a nightmare, a war zone. That's right, it's war! And I'll not stand here like some pathetic pacifist while the commander and his squadrons of Ritalin addicts add me to their death count. I'm fighting back! (*Calling*) *Ahhhhh, toro, mira, toro, ahhhh.* Throw the ball, cheesehead! I've read Hemingway's *Death in the Afternoon*, and if I must fight, (*Striking a pose*) I will fight with dignity . . . without fear. And if you gouge me, I will not show surprise or anguish. No more jerky little movements because . . . I am elegance and beauty. The essence of rhythm and grace, the matador! (*Dodging the ball*) *Olé!* Aha! Your little ball missed me. Weenies! Before you engage in the *corrida de toros*, a complete bullfight with a real matador, perhaps you and your little boys should practice with the *novillada*, the amateurs in middle school. *Ahhhhh, toro, mira, toro, ahhhh.* (*Dodging*) Aha! You missed again! And now I will defeat you with a very basic pass, the *veronica*. (*He is the matador*) Holding my cape so gently by the corners, as if wiping the face of Jesus on the Cross, I will cite, pass, and complete this move. *Ahhhhh, toro, mira, toro, ahhhh. Olé!* Ha, ha, ha! And now the *hora de la verdad*, the hour of truth. And when I am done, I will cut off the bull's testicles, I will roast them on an open fire, and I will eat them. Yummy! *Ahhhhh, toro, mira, toro.* Lifting my *muleta* and concealing the *matar*, I will not stand, *recibiendo*, and wait for the bull to charge. No, my friend, I will charge the waiting bull, *volapie*, and with flying feet, I will run like hell to the locker room. Wait! What do you know? Ha, ha, ha. There is fear in the bull's eyes. See it? Yes . . . fear. He knows now that he is defeated. *Olé*!

End of Scene

from BOTTOM'S DREAM

Scene

A high-school baseball game. George Bottom, an overly expressive fan, sits in the bleachers.

GEORGE BOTTOM: (*Encouraging the pitcher*) Come on, Jake, come on, you gotta fight back now, and get 'em. Hard! Rock and fire! Pop! Oh, mother of God! Whew! And that's three! Yeah, daddy! (*The batter throws down his bat*) Hey! Hey! He can't do that! (*Yelling at the umpire*) Hey, fat boy, he can't do that! That's unsportsmanlike. He can't do that, fat boy! Toss his skinny butt out of the park! (*Surprised by the umpire*) What? Don't tell me to take it easy. Do your job, fat boy, and take control of this situation! Someone's gonna get hurt! And it just might be you! (*To the pitcher*) This one likes to bunt, Jake! Don't give it to him! Rock and fire! Pop! (*A strike*) That a boy! Make him stand tall and take the heat like the rest of 'em. Come on, now. Two more. Mix it up! (*Another strike*) Oh, yeah! Slap! That was pretty, boy. Snappy, sweet, and smooth. Right, here we go, here we go, here . . . we . . . Pop! (*Strike three*) He's outta here! Two down and one to go! Make it one to go! Make it one to go! Hey, fat boy . . . make it . . . one to go! (*To the pitcher*) Watch it now. He likes the inside and he's a sucker for a high one. Just give 'em your stuff. Rock and fire! And it's . . . (*Strike one*) one! Slap leather! Pretty pitch! The kid's a dream. Two more and let's go home! Pull back, stretch, and throw hard. Give him a big target, Catch. (*Strike two*) Pop. Slap leather. And it's . . . two! A dream. All right. (*To the pitcher*) Now, here we go. Rock and fire! Yeah! Nice pitch! What?! (*Incredulously*) A ball? Did he say a ball?! (*Yelling at the umpire*) You are a horse's ass, fat boy. A fat jackass that needs glasses! You wouldn't know a strike if it hit you between the jackass eyes, fat boy! (*Rising*) What? You can't throw me out! You can't stop the game like this. The game is bigger than you, fat boy. Put on that mask, squat down a few inches, if you can, and call the strike. (*Slight pause*) Well . . . you gonna do it? (*He sits*) No . . . we'll just sit here then. We'll just sit right here. We'll just see.

End of Scene

from FIE UPON'T!

Scene

A theater. Henri's assistant stage manager has been told he will perform as an understudy.

HENRI: (*Instructing*) Exhale . . . damn it! You can do this. You've been my assistant . . . assistant stage manager since the beginning. (*With growing frustration*) You know every word, every movement, every pause, and every . . . thing . . . because . . . I taught you. (*Uncontrollably*) I taught you . . . everything, and now . . . you will walk out there . . . to applause . . . and once again, I . . . will . . . not. And . . . I admit . . . it hurts. (*Exclaiming*) *Stop the World, I Want to Get Off*! Oh, if the director had only seen me in that show . . . he would know . . . yes . . . he would know. (*Venting his emotions*) "Fie upon't! Foh!" I'm just a little upset that the director asked you and not me to take over this role. I'm sorry, but what experience have you had? (*Reaching Hamlet's emotional conclusion*) "What would he do had he the motive and the cue for passion that I have?" I mean, you're a first-year student, and I've been a member of the Studio for almost three years . . . if you count summer stock . . . which I do. I've paid my dues and even adopted a stage name, Henri with an "i". It's just not fair. Inhale. (*He does*) "Fie upon't!" (*Letting loose*) I know he doesn't like me. He has his pet actors. I think he's sleeping with Ophelia . . . oh, it makes me mad. And if I complain, I'll never be cast. You see, I can say nothing. Except, "Bloody, bawdy villain! Remorseless, treacherous, lecherous, kindless villain!" There. Exhale. (*Regaining control*) Whew! I feel better now. I'm sorry you had to hear that . . . but if you act around here . . . I mean, if you are going to be an actor in this theater . . . you must learn to perform . . . fearlessly . . . boldly . . . and without a net. And remember what the flying Karl Wallenda said: "The dead are gone, and the show must go on." So, places . . . and . . . break a leg!

End of Scene

from REIN IN THE STERLING SPHINXES

Scene

A small-town parade. Mitchell Gray and a friend have entered a float in the parade in hopes of winning the competition. He stops the float at the judges' station and steps out to deliver his prepared speech for the judges.

MITCHELL GRAY: (*Reciting his speech with mechanical precision*) We celebrate this day, during the annual Popcorn Day Festival, honoring a tradition that started thousands of years ago: the parade of the ancient procession of the god Up-wa-wet. Like all who have paraded, yesterday and today, we move in a straight line, very slowly, so as not to bump into each other. My friend and I have put on a great show to celebrate the parade's theme: "The Past Meets the Future: Say Hooray for Popcorn Day!" (*Ceremoniously*) Up-wa-wet, we praise thee, and, we thank the city fathers and these smart judges for this opportunity to display our float, designed by Newton and Gray. Hooray for Popcorn Day! (*Guiding the judges*) Please note: Our float is truly a float. It isn't pulled by animals, like those that have gone before us, or by tractors, like those that will follow. Ours . . . really . . . floats. (*Instructing*) Note how it glides, effortlessly, graciously, onward, as these two shiny Egyptian sphinxes, harnessed to this silver NASA rocket, all surrounded by a metallic heat shield, and all made completely of recycled aluminum foil and chicken wire, connect the myths of our past to the mysteries of our future. Hooray for Popcorn Day! (*With humility*) And thank you. Judges, we hope you are pleased with our entry.

End of Scene

from THE LINE-UP (MONOLOG ONE)

Scene

A theater. Barry Gascon, an ex-con, walks conspicuously onto the stage to audition.

BARRY GASCON: (*Clearing his throat, Barry talks directly to the casting directors in the audience*) Okay, now, ahh . . . the rosy spandex girl . . . there . . . in the wings . . . with the clipboard . . . and the nice muffins . . . said . . . I'm . . . ahh . . . supposed to say my name first and then this . . . here number. (*Referring to a number pinned to his shirt*) Is that right? (*Nodding*) Well . . . the name is . . . Barry Gascon. And I'm . . . ahh . . . (*checking his number*) numero twenty-five. So there. (*All business*) Let's get something straight here. I don't belong to the lavender club. I mean, if I'm gonna engage in a little tongue sushi today . . . it's going to be with the rosy spandex girl and not with none of you yodelers. I don't yodel . . . and . . . I don't dance . . . well . . . that ain't exactly true. I do dance a little . . . you know, "Rompin' Molly" or that . . . ahh . . . "Pigtown Hoe Down," but I need a lot of room for that, so that's another story. To be honest with you, I've never done nothin' like this before . . . and so if you don't want me . . . just do a little preemptive strike here . . . it won't break my heart. I belong to the Union. I have friends. I'm walkin' tall. It ain't like I'm just dyin' to be here . . . you know. No . . . it ain't an obsession . . . with me. I'm here today because . . . well . . . (*Not too happy about this*) my parole officer said, "Barry, you're goin' to do some community service when you get out." Well, I ain't pickin' up garbage or watchin' some old fart drool at the old geezers' home . . . but when I saw your announcement . . . about community theater . . . I asked my parole officer, "Hey, do you think . . . community theater is community service?" (*Shrugging*) And since he didn't have a good answer . . . I'm here.

End of Scene

from THE LINE-UP (MONOLOG TWO)

Scene

A theater. Barry Gascon, an ex-con, walks conspicuously onto the stage to audition.

BARRY GASCON: (*Barry talks directly to the casting director in the audience*) I'm . . . ahh . . . (*Checking his number*) numero twenty-five. I'm here today because . . . well . . . my parole officer said, "Barry, you're goin' to do some community service when you get out." Well, I ain't pickin' up garbage or watchin' some old fart drool at the old geezers' home . . . but when I saw your announcement . . . about community theater . . . I asked my parole officer, "Hey, do you think community theater is community service?" (*Shrugging*) And since he didn't have a good answer, I'm here. But . . . ahh . . . he said I would have to read somethin' or recite somethin', and I noticed the actor before me, number twenty-four, was like . . . acting his cojones off. I mean, I really thought he was gonna beat up on that girl he was acting with . . . here. And when he started yellin' (*Imitating the actor*) "Stella! Stella!" It looked like he was gonna upchuck right here on the floor! (*Total disbelief*) Right here! Mother Mary! (*Startled*) Look-a here! There is a puddle of sweat right here on the stage floor! The guy must have been sweatin' like a horse . . . I mean, you saw him, right? (*Heavily involved*) He looked like an animal. And the way he growled (*Growling*), "Stella!" It sent chills right down my spine . . . and into my flat feet. Listen to me, I know. I've seen fireworks in my time . . . but nothin' . . . was more thrillin' than that moment. (*Emphatically*) That man is an actor! You should use him. Listen to me! But now it's gone! All that emotion . . . is just a memory! And what did he leave behind? This puddle of sweat! (*Slight pause*) Wait a minute! You don't think the girl peed herself, do you? Naaah, it's sweat. The man is an actor! You know, you gotta use him in this production. (*Taking over*) You got his phone number?

His line-up number was ... ahh ... twenty-four ... and his name was Marvin or Stanley. Listen, I'll do you a favor. I'll call him back out here. (*Shouting*) Hey, Chum! Marvin! Stanley! (*Looking in the wings*) Guess he's gone. Too bad. Hey, you know, I kinda' like this theater thing. Standing up here ... on the stage ... shoutin' ... at the top of my voice. It kinda frees you up, you know, what they call ... therapeutic. Makes you feel good. Tell you what. Go ahead. Sign me up. I'll do your play. And now, as a bonus, I'm gonna do a little "Rompin' Molly," or maybe you'd rather see my "Pigtown Hoe Down." They're both good. (*He dances*)

End of scene

Chapter 7

from SHORTY'S OLD MAN'S BOARD OR S'UP?

Scene
Downtown parking lot. Slick, a teenage boy, glides onto the scene on his skateboard with great dexterity and skill.

SLICK: (*Catching his breath*) Whoa, did you see the news? City passed a law against boarders. Said the cops can ticket us, man, if they catch us on public property, like right here and now, downtown. I say, let 'em try to catch us. (*Playfully*) We'd smoke 'em, flip, slide, and glide away. (*Checking out his friend's board*) But not on that thing. Not on Shorty's old man's board. The thing is ass-out dangerous, with those metal skates, you know what I mean? You hit just a little rock, dude, like a pebble, and the skate will nose grind and flip your ass back to the future. I am not kidding, Newt. I wouldn't do it. (*Shaking his head*) Well, yeah, I know you're like . . . (*Imitating Newt*) "Nothing can happen to me, man, I know every crack in the concrete, every bump in the road. Like it's my cosmic highway I ride all day, every day, dude, eternal and never changing." It's like Newt's laws of skateboarding motion. (*Startled by Newt's movement toward the top of the hill*) Wait! No way, man! Not down Nollie's Hill, dude. Not now, man, it's rush hour, and not unless you have a high tolerance for pain. Not unless you're a camel or somethin', 'cause you gonna die, dude, if you do that! You hear me? You gonna die! And I'll have to go knock on your door (*Rapping on his board*), and your old lady, wringing her hands on a wash towel, will answer: "He ain't here, Slick." And I'll have to say, "You're telling me! The last time I saw him, he tried an indy grab down Nollie's Hill, and now he's, like, road kill or something, with ten toes up!" She gets all whacked and emotional and starts dissing on me about boarders, and I don't need to hear that from your old lady, Newt. (*Trying to assert himself*) So give me the board, Newt. Give it here. (*Demanding*) You can't ride it down Nollie, and that's it!

End of Scene

Chapter 7

from STYLING WITH WILLIAM

Scene

A cafeteria in a student union building. Rosen, a student, has just returned from an unsuccessful meeting with his literature professor.

ROSEN: "It's all in your head," he said. I'm flunking the class, and he tells me, "It's all in my head!" He won't give me an extension. "No extensions," he snapped. "If Napoleon could greet thousands of his soldiers by name, you should be able to recite one of Shakespeare's little speeches." The man's a tyrant, Newton, and I fart at him and his old English! And I'm sick of his class. (*Slamming the book shut*) And I'm sick of this school! I'm sick of it! Hell, I'd rather skateboard to the nearest McJob and spend my off time rewinding *Oprah*. (*Rising*) I'm sick of his insults . . . his academic terrorism . . . making me feel . . . like dog shit, like bio-hazard, like something . . . unworthy. That's it! (*Fully and expressively*) Like the man said, "How unworthy a thing you make of me! You would play upon me, you would seem to know my stops, you would pluck out the heart of my mystery, you would sound me from my lowest note to the top of my compass—and there is much music, excellent voice, in this little organ—yet cannot you make it speak. 'Sblood, do you think I am easier to be played on than a pipe? Call me what instrument you will; though you can fret me, you cannot play upon me." (*Amazed—sitting*) Gawd! I did it! That's it. I know the speech. I know it! I don't need an extension, I'm busting on the scene and I need an audience. I just blurted it out! You heard it. Out! Out . . . of . . . my brain and my heart, and for a moment I felt down with Hamlet, in tune with the man . . . styling! Styling with William! Let the class begin!

End of Scene

Hamlet, Act III, sc. ii, lines 380–390.

from HALLEY'S FAT STRAT

Scene

A rock 'n' roll stage. Eddie is laying cable, connecting microphones, and testing the sound levels before the evening's concert.

EDDIE HALLEY: (*Speaking into a microphone*) Check. Check. This is Eddie Halley . . . testing, sliding on a moonbeam. Testing. One, two. Check. (*Talking to a lighting technician working a follow spot*) Hey! We're tweaking the levels on these three mics, and then you can run your lights. Testing, one, two, check. Mic number one, check. "Chuck Berry is here to stay"—testing. "And when he plays that Johnny song,"—testing, "my air guitar begins to sway." (*Playing the air guitar to "Johnny B. Good"*) So, "Go, go, Johnny, go, go, go, de, de, de, de, de. Go, Johnny, go, go, go." (*He stops suddenly and moves to the next microphone*) Aaahrightie, that's smooth, let's lay down a groove on mic number two. Hey, did I tell you? The band offered me a tour with 'em . . . as a roadie. It's cool! I dig this band and I like their music . . . it's more booty-shaking then head-banging . . . which is good, 'cause I'm growin' out of the metalhead period in my life. Besides, they've got one bad-ass guitarist . . . Louie. You just wait till you hear him tonight. I swear, he shreds the ass off of that beautiful '57 Fiesta Red Fat Strat he wears. And what passion! Man, where can you learn that? (*Working it out*) But it means I . . . ah . . . won't be goin' back to school next fall, but . . . ah . . . that's okay, because, well, the dean and I didn't seem to agree on the meanin' of my GPA. Okay, here we go. (*Checking the second microphone*) Check. Testing, mic number two. This is Eddie Halley, awake but walkin' in a purple haze. "Jimi Hendrix is dead and gone,"—testing, "but his memory lingers on"—testing. "When his mood was one of bliss,"—testing, "he wrote crushin' tunes like this." (*Playing his air guitar to Hendrix's version of*

"*The Star Spangled Banner*") De, de, de, de, dede, de dewangg. De, de, de, de, dede, de, dewingg. (*He stops playing and prepares to test the third microphone*) Aaahrightie, let's move on to number three.

End of Scene

from THE BIG BANG

Scene

A recital hall. Thurston, a free-spirited drummer, is one of several percussionists asked to participate in the state orchestra concert.

THURSTON: (*Standing next to the gong*) Why did I agree to do this? I mean, look at all these music geeks—flutes, cellos, violas. This orchestra stuff is too weird. You know me, I'm strictly rock 'n' roll. I feel like I should take off my shirt when I play the skins; instead I'm standing here in a penguin suit . . . waiting for the conductor-man to point at me so that I can smash this gong with a mallet. (*Amused*) Hey, and look at you, dude. They've got you dingin' a little triangle. Dinga, dinga, dinga. Isn't that precious? You know, I thought people only wore tuxedos at weddings or to the Oscars, or, you know, when they crowned a new president, that kind of thing. But this is tight-ass music, I mean, "bottle up that fart, man, cause it isn't getting' out tonight" kind of music. (*Pointing out the conductor*) Hey, and did you catch the conductor, know what I mean? That dude is serious. I hear he's from England—some music conservatory. (*Gestures toward the other percussionist*) And look, Newton, look at the Waldo playing the kettle drum . . . the timpani. Man, he looks like he can barely lift those sticks. He must weigh in at sixty-five pounds. He should be dingin' the triangle, you should be bangin' this gong, and I should be rippin' on the skins. I know it's suppose to be an honor . . . state orchestra . . . all that . . . but it's weird. Can't wait till it's over. (*Sizing up the situation*) And why do we have to stand way back here where no one can see us? We should be in the middle and all these musical yahoos should surround us. The most important sound, percussion, should take center stage, Newton. Am I right? I'm goin' to complain to the conductor. (*Starts to call out*) Hey, Maestro! (*To his friend*) Too late. He's liftin' his little stick. Here we go. Rock 'n' roll.

End of Scene

from THE PIANO TUNER (MONOLOG ONE)

Scene

An empty stage, with the exception of maybe a piano tucked into the corner.

TONY: I could never audition for people. Honest to God, it makes my stomach bounce just saying the word "audition." But my sister, Theresa, Newt, she was a triple threat. She could sing, dance, act . . . she did it all. I don't know why some Broadway agent didn't scoop her up. She was an artist . . . a real triple threat. (*Changing the subject*) Okay, the piano is ready, Newt. If they move it too much, I should have to tune it again. And I . . . ahh . . . located the reason for that vibration. It was a wad of bubble gum . . . under the sound-board. Honest to God, I don't understand why anyone would treat a work of art . . . like that . . . by throwing a wad of disgusting gum garbage in it! (*With growing irritation*) To me, it's like someone defacing the face of Mona Lisa or carving his initials in the Vietnam Veterans Memorial. They don't deserve to touch it or even be near it. What is it with these people? Don't they know, Newt, that art is rare . . . like the best of our dreams? . . Newt, like my sister, Theresa, the triple threat, who would have loved to audition here . . . but . . . is . . . no longer. Honest to God, Newt, if we are ever to know heaven here on earth, we must take care of the artist and . . . and . . . her instrument. (*He pauses*) I'm sorry, Newt. I didn't mean to preach to you. I . . . guess . . . I'm feeling a little . . . ahh . . . I don't know . . . emotional . . . today. On this stage. (*Nodding his head*) Well, yeah, I guess auditions start soon . . . so . . . ahh . . . you light them well, Newt. Make their faces shine bright. And I hope all these kids auditioning here this afternoon find work. I hope they all get to sing and act and dance. And I'd consider it a privilege to tune their pianos on Broadway ... some day ... or even next door at the little theater. (*Collecting his tools*) So, anyway, you tell 'em that that piano has great action; she's in first-class condition. I've ... ahh ... set the temperament ... and ... ahh ... if they treat her well, she will play.

End of Scene

from THE PIANO TUNER (MONOLOG TWO)

Scene

An empty stage, with the exception of maybe a piano tucked into the corner.

TONY: (*Directing his voice to the top of the theater*) The piano is tuned. Hey, Newt, did ya hear me? I tuned that piano . . . for the auditions this afternoon? (*Shaking his head*) If they move it too much, I should have to tune it again. And I . . . ahh . . . located the reason for that vibration. We call it . . . ahh . . . "sympathetic rattle" in the tuning profession. She ain't cracked, thank God, or split, or anything like that. It was a piece . . . of . . . candy . . . or a wad of bubble gum . . . under the soundboard. Can you believe that, Newt? (*Reaching into his toolbox*) And I got the candy out with this piece of hickory stick. Honest to God, I don't understand why anyone would treat a work of art . . . this instrument of the gods . . . like that . . . by throwing a wad of disgusting gum garbage in it! (*With growing irritation*) To me, it's like someone defacing the face of Mona Lisa or carving his initials in the Vietnam Veterans Memorial. They don't deserve to touch it or even be near it. What is it with these people? Don't they know, Newt, that art is rare . . . like the best of our dreams? (*Slight pause*) Honest to God, Newt, if we are ever to know heaven here on earth, we must take care of the artist and her instrument. (*Slight pause*) I'm sorry, Newt. I didn't mean to preach to you. I know it's not your fault. That piano has great action; she's in first-class condition. I've . . . ahh . . . set the temperament . . . and . . . ahh . . . if they treat her well, she will play. (*He starts to leave*) Oh, yeah, I left the bill on the piano. They need to pay it in ten days.

End of Scene

8 THE NEWTON MONOLOG PROJECT IN PERFORMANCE

THE MONOLOGS IN THIS BOOK may be used as material for classroom scene study, auditions, or a performance—an evening of theater. The selection and arrangement of the monologs for an evening of theater largely depends on the talents of the actors, the length of the performance, and the level of production, ranging from a bare stage to a fully realized design concept.

As an evening of theater, many of these monologs were first performed on October 2, 2002, at the Ball Theater on the Wabash College campus. The company of actors included Christina Holmstrom, Suzie David, Chris Laguna, Jamie Ritchie-Watson, Janathan Grandoit, Matt McKay, Richard Winters, Alexandra Hudson, Christopher Mehl, Nikki Perry, Edward Conley, and Reynaldo Pacheco. Luke Elliott and Donald Claxon served as stage managers, and Denis Farr as assistant director. Laura Conners, costume designer, and James Gross, scene and lighting designer, enlivened all aspects of the visual production. The performance was divided into two parts, with one ten-minute intermission. The design involved a series of elevated circular platforms and circles of light, defining a space for each monolog. The performance began with the actor who portrayed a piano tuner, Tony, in the last monolog of the evening, *The Piano Tuner*, as he tuned a piano and prepared the theater for the audition and/or performance that was to follow.

The monologs in this book are protected by copyright. It is, however, fair use of these monologs for audition or for instructional purposed related to the classroom. All dramatic, production, or film rights are strictly reserved. For additional information, please contact the author at Wabash College, P.O. Box 352, Crawfordsville, IN 47933 or at watsond@wabash.edu.

9 PROPERTY AND COSTUME PLOT

BIRTH OF A STAR
Princess Ipia: Pants, shirt, jacket, shoes
1—Flower arrangement

BON VOYAGE
Alissa: Swimsuit or lightweight pants, shirt with lifeguard logo, no shoes
1—Lifeguard whistle
Sun gear (zinc salve, suntan lotion)
1—Hairbrush
1—Beach towel

HOOFER
Zenith Blacketer: Dancewear—leotard, tights, skirt
1—Shoulder bag with bottled water, chips, candy, tap shoe, and sheet music for "Sweet Georgia Brown"

TRACTORS AND TWIRLERS
Julie Stalbird: Jeans, festive shirt
1—Baton (optional)
1—Bag of confetti (optional)

ODE TO LITTLE AUDREY

Audrey: Dress, tie-up sneakers

1—Jump rope

HUMMERS, ROCKETS, AND SPLIT COMETS

Shelley: Summer shorts, hiking shoes, Fourth of July shirt

1—Blanket

F = WD

Sarah: Sweatshirt with college logo, jeans

1—Calculus textbook

STAGE FRIGHT PIANOLOGUE

Nicole: Dress, jacket with pockets, scarf

1—Sheet music (for musicals)

1—Pad with names of those auditioning

BUCKAROO BELLE AND THE BULL RIDER

Katie Belle: Dungarees, belt buckle, chaps, western boots

1—"Bull" exercise barrel (or a stool)

1—Saddle for the barrel (optional)

CHOCOLATE THIN MINTS

Virginia Dare: Sweatshirt with college logo, jeans or skirt

1—Backpack

THE TWILIGHT ARCH

Torrie: Jeans, sweatshirt or top, outdoor shoes

1—Blanket

LIZZIE'S LILLIPUT

Lizzie: Skirt, blouse, dress shoes

Nerf toys (sword, etc.)

TWO BLUSHING PILGRIMS
Kari: Jeans or overalls, jacket or sweater, tennis shoes
3—Bags of supplies (containing theatrical items—not necessarily seen)

HARD KNOCKS
Darcy Wells: "Annie" dress and shoes
1—Clipboard
1—Name tag for Darcy Wells

HEAD SHOTS AND HOT BUTTERED BISCUITS
Charlotta: Skirt or stretch pants, leotard, black boots, scarf
1—(or more) 8" x 10" head shots/résumés of Charlotta

BEAST BALLET
Renee: Dance warm-up/rehearsal clothes
1—Stool

A LEAN, MEAN, SINGING MACHINE
Otto Gunther: Slacks, turtleneck, sport coat, dress shoes
1—*Messiah* sheet music
1—Music stand (optional)
1—Baton (optional)

PETER PAN AND THE SQUARE-RIGGER
Joel: Overalls, T-shirt
1—Coil of rope with block and tackle

A SEAMLESS PITCH
Allen: Jeans or shorts, short shirt, tennis shoes
1—Baseball (optional)

THE 1ST DEAD MAN IN GROVER'S CORNERS

1st Dead Man: Two-piece dark suit, shirt and tie,
dress shoes
4—Straight-back wooden chairs
3—Black umbrellas

DODGEBALL MATADOR

Adam: Gym shorts, P.E. T-shirt, school logo, gym shoes
1—Gym towel (to use as cape)

BOTTOM'S DREAM

George Bottom: Pants, T-shirt with baseball logo, tennis shoes
1—Baseball glove
1—Bag of popcorn (optional)

FIE UPON'T!

Henri: Black slacks, black turtleneck, black shoes
1—Clipboard with notes

REIN IN THE STERLING SPHINXES

Mitchell Gray: Silver/gray coveralls with reflector tape;
aluminum-foil helmet
1—Straight-back wooden chair
1—Platform to represent the parade float

THE LINE-UP

Barry Gascon: Work pants, short-sleeve shirt or tank top,
work shoes
1—Audition number (25) pinned to Barry's shirt

SHORTY'S OLD MAN'S BOARD OR S'UP?

Slick: Oversize pants, T-shirt with skateboarding logo, skateboarding shoes
1—Skateboard

STYLING WITH WILLIAM
Rosen: Cargo pants, T-shirt, tennis shoes
1—Backpack
1—Metal chair
1—Book of Shakespeare

HALLEY'S FAT STRAT
Eddie Halley: Jeans, T-shirt with rock music logo
3—Microphones
3—Microphone stands
Cable for each microphone

THE BIG BANG
Thurston: Tuxedo, formal shirt and tie, black dress shoes
1—Gong
1—Mallet
1—Sheet music (classical)
1—Music stand

THE PIANO TUNER
Tony: Pants, work shirt, work shoes
1—Piano tuner tool box w/tools
1—Piece of hickory stick

About the Author

Dwight Watson has been an active member of the academic and artistic community for more than twenty-five years. He has directed over sixty productions for educational and professional theaters. He has received a number of playwriting awards and grants, and his work appears in several anthologies. Currently, he is a Professor of Theater and serves as Chair of the Division of Humanities and Fine Arts at Wabash College.

Books from Allworth Press

Allworth Press is an imprint of Allworth Communications, Inc. Selected titles are listed below.

Creating Your Own Monologue, Second Edition
by Glenn Alterman (paperback, 6 × 9, 256 pages, $19.95)

Acting—Advanced Techniques for the Actor, Director, and Teacher
by Terry Schreiber (paperback, 6 × 9, 256 pages, $19.95)

How to Audition for TV Commercials: From the Ad Agency Point of View
by W.L. Jenkins (paperback, 6 × 9, 208 pages, $16.95)

Improv for Actors
by Dan Diggles (paperback, 6 × 9, 246 pages, $19.95)

Movement for Actors
edited by Nicole Potter (paperback, 6 × 9, 288 pages, $19.95)

Acting for Film
by Cathy Haase (paperback, 6 × 9, 224 pages, $19.95)

Acting That Matters
by Barry Pineo (paperback, 6 × 9, 240 pages, $16.95)

Mastering Shakespeare: An Acting Class in Seven Scenes
by Scott Kaiser (paperback, 6 × 9, 246 pages, $19.95)

The Art of Auditioning
by Rob Decina (paperback, 6 × 9, 224 pages, $19.95)

An Actor's Guide—Making It in New York City
by Glenn Alterman (paperback, 6 × 9, 288 pages, $19.95)

Promoting Your Acting Career
by Glenn Alterman (paperback, 6 × 9, 224 pages, $18.95)

The Health and Safety Guide for Film, TV and Theater
by Monona Rossol (paperback, 6 × 9, 256 pages, $19.95)

Please write to request our free catalog. To order by credit card, call 1-800-491-2808 or send a check or money order to Allworth Press, 10 East 23rd Street, Suite 510, New York, NY 10010. Include $5 for shipping and handling for the first book ordered and $1 for each additional book. Ten dollars plus $1 for each additional book if ordering from Canada. New York State residents must add sales tax.

To see our complete catalog on the World Wide Web, or to order online, you can find us at
www.allworth.com.